The

UNƎXPECTED
EVOLUTION
of
LANGUAGE

The

UNEXPECTED

EVOLUTION

of

LANGUAGE

Discover *the*
SURPRISING
ETYMOLOGY
of Everyday
WORDS

JUSTIN CORD HAYES

SPINSTER

ORIGINAL DEFINITION:
a woman who spins thread

NEW DEFINITION: a woman who
remains single beyond the
typical age for marrying

BANDWAGON

ORIGINAL DEFINITION: circus wagon carrying
a band

NEW DEFINITION: a movement, often political,
with a lot of support

ABACK

ORIGINAL DEFINITION: at or on
the back; backward

NEW DEFINITION: by surprise
(with "taken")

*To all the authors and teachers who inspired
my love of languages, and to my family.*

Published by
Adams Media, a division of F+W Media, Inc.
57 Littlefield Street, Avon, MA 02322. U.S.A.
www.adamsmedia.com

ISBN 10: 1-4405-4278-3
ISBN 13: 978-1-4405-4278-7
eISBN 10: 1-4405-4279-1
eISBN 13: 978-1-4405-4279-4

Printed in the United States of America.

10   9   8   7   6   5   4   3   2   1

Library of Congress Cataloging-in-Publication Data
Hayes, Justin Cord.
 The unexpected evolution of language / Justin Cord Hayes.
   p. cm.
 ISBN 978-1-4405-4278-7 (pbk.) – ISBN 1-4405-4278-3 (pbk.) – ISBN 978-1-4405-
4279-4 (ebook) – ISBN 1-4405-4279-1 (ebook)
1. English language–Etymology. 2. English language–History. I. Title.
 PE1574.H39 2012
 422–dc23

                         2012024255

This publication is designed to provide accurate and authoritative information with
regard to the subject matter covered. It is sold with the understanding that the pub-
lisher is not engaged in rendering legal, accounting, or other professional advice.
If legal advice or other expert assistance is required, the services of a competent
professional person should be sought.
            —From a *Declaration of Principles* jointly adopted by a Committee of the
      American Bar Association and a Committee of Publishers and Associations

Many of the designations used by manufacturers and sellers to distinguish their
product are claimed as trademarks. Where those designations appear in this book
and Adams Media was aware of a trademark claim, the designations have been
printed with initial capital letters.

*This book is available at quantity discounts for bulk purchases.
For information, please call 1-800-289-0963.*

Introduction

English is the mutt, the Heinz 57, the bastard child of every language that came before it. That's why it's so inscrutable to those who encounter it after learning their well-behaved, logical languages. Our words trace gnarly roots that sometimes dead end, and we're certainly not averse to coining words that have no roots or reason at all. ("Hornswoggle," anyone?)

It's those gnarly roots that you'll find in this book. Some of the English words you *think* you're familiar with actually used to mean something quite different. How on earth does a definition just change, you ask? Well, it depends. The definitions of the words in this book were twisted due to historical events, cultural adjustments, or technological advancements. The fascinating stories behind these transformations are surprising (see entry for "stadium"), thoughtful (see entry for "acquit"), and sometimes pretty funny (see entry for "occupy"). One thing to keep in mind is that "English" is really three Englishes: old, middle, and modern. Ask most people which one was Shakespeare's purview, and they'll say, "Oh, he wrote in Middle English." Nope, sorry. He wrote in Modern English. Don't let all those "forsooths," "cozes," and "fiddlesticks" throw you off.

Before we get started, it's helpful to know a little bit about the origins of the English language. Old English lasted from roughly A.D. 700 to about A.D. 1100. The grammar of Old English was closely related to Latin. Old English, also called Anglo-Saxon, was spoken by the . . . Anglo-Saxons. These were Germanic tribes who invaded and then settled in portions of what is today Great Britain.

Old English is indecipherable to us today; it's basically a "foreign" language. Nonetheless, we do have surviving Old English texts such as *Caedmon's Hymn*. This nine-line poem written in honor of God is the acorn (see entry for "acorn") from which has grown the mighty oak of literature in English. Written around A.D. 700, it's the oldest piece of English literature known to exist. Old English also is the language of the epic *Beowulf* . . . .

For all intents and purposes, Old English ended with the famous Norman Conquest. The Normans were French and defeated the English, the erstwhile Anglo-Saxons, at the Battle of Hastings on October 14, 1066. Middle English survived until the 1400s. It's the language of Geoffrey Chaucer, author of the immortal *The Canterbury Tales*. Though it's written in Middle English, most people today can read and understand those stories, as long as the text contains plenty of footnotes.

Middle English shifted to Modern English when many in England adopted the Chancery Standard, a form of English spoken in London. The standard was adapted, in part, because of the printing press, introduced to England around 1470. Thus, Modern English took over by the 1500s and holds sway today. It's the language of everything from Shakespeare to Dickens to Hawthorne to Dickinson to Faulkner to all those annoying bloggers who can't spell.

Modern English rose at the time of great world exploration and is now the polyglot stew we know and usually love (but sometimes abhor). Perhaps due to its "mutt-like" origins, we English speakers continue to coin words and phrases with a frequency that would have shocked Chaucer . . . and probably even Shakespeare.

With centuries of history under its belt, maybe it's not so surprising that English words have changed meanings over the years. Sometimes, we easily can trace why a word once meant "this" but now means "that"; yet, at other times, the only things to rely on are common sense and speculation based on historical trends.

What follows are about 200 words that used to mean one thing and now mean something else. Some of them have changed in logical, sensible ways, while others have undergone the linguistic equivalent of complete reconstructive surgery—shifting, for example, from a verb to a noun or vice versa—bringing them to the point where even these words' mothers wouldn't recognize them. But what do you expect from a language that's the semantic cross between a Dutch elm, an oak, and a Japanese maple?

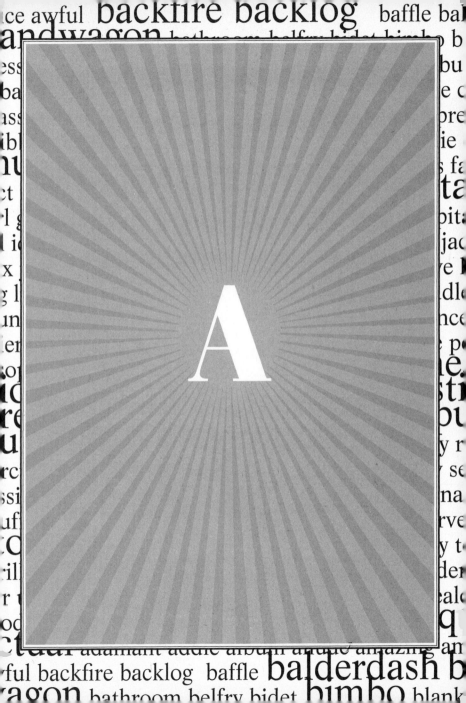

aback

A

ORIGINAL DEFINITION: at or on the back; backward
NEW DEFINITION: by surprise (with "taken")

You're most familiar with this word from the expression "taken aback." Come to think of it . . . do you *ever* hear the word without "taken" as its partner? When the word first popped up, in the middle of the Middle Ages, you might have.

For example, you might have carried your wares "aback," meaning "on your back." Or the wind might have been "aback," meaning "at your back." These seem like perfectly reasonable uses of the word "aback," but they lost favor completely by the middle of the nineteenth century.

The word as we know it today—as part of the expression "taken aback"—came about for nautical reasons. When finicky winds change direction quickly, boats' sails can "deflate" and hang limply back onto the ship's mast. Eventually, sailors began to refer to this condition as being "taken aback."

One hundred years later, the expression became metaphorical. After all, you can imagine that wind suddenly changing direction for no apparent reason was surprising and dismaying. By extension, anytime you are "taken aback," you are surprised and dismayed.

abode

ORIGINAL DEFINITION: delay; act of waiting
NEW DEFINITION: formal word for one's home

The words "abode" and "abide" spring from the same source. In fact, from the 1200s to the 1500s, they meant the same thing— "wait," "withstand," or "tolerate." The words were connected

A

because of the manner in which Old English verbs were conjugated: "Abode" was a past tense version of "abide."

Then, during the 1500s and 1600s, "abide" still meant "wait," "withstand," or "tolerate," while "abode" changed to refer to one's home. One reason for the change is metaphorical. If you think about it, people spend a lot of time waiting at home. In the sixteenth century, people waited for dinner to be slaughtered, for wool to be spun into coats, and for the kids to come home from whatever bad stuff they were doing. Today, people wait for their favorite TV show to come on, and for the kids to come home from whatever bad stuff they're doing. As people "aboded" in their homes, they just began to refer to their dwellings as abodes.

The modern, mostly European, concept of "right of abode" captures both the old and new meanings of the word. The "right" allows people to be free from immigration authorities and to have a right to work and live in a particular country. Thus, they can "wait" as long as they like in a nation, and have an "abode" there as well.

accentuate

ORIGINAL DEFINITION: to pronounce with an accent
NEW DEFINITION: to emphasize

Our world's increasingly polyglot nature led to the change in the word "accentuate." Originally, it meant "to pronounce with an accent." As cultures and their respective languages mingled, people had to work extra hard to be understood. As a result, they spoke carefully so that people could understand their "accentuated" (spoken with an accent) words. Thus, it's not much of a leap for the word to shift from "speaking with an accent" to carefully

A

"emphasizing" each word so that other people can understand what you're saying.

After the shift occurred, "accentuate" began to mean "emphasize." By the middle of the nineteenth century, "accentuate" had all but lost its original meaning. In writing, "accentuate" means to mark with written accents. For example, if you're writing out the meter of a poem, you use accentuating marks to indicate how to "scan lines" (analyze them rhythmically).

---

accolade

ORIGINAL DEFINITION: ceremony conferring knighthood
NEW DEFINITION: praise; expression of approval

From a Latin word meaning "to embrace around the neck," an accolade used to include this actual action. An accolade was a formal ceremony that conferred knighthood on a worthy wight (person).

The ceremony went something like this. Royalty would embrace the knight-to-be about the neck, kiss him, and tap his shoulders with a sword. Even today, children still mimic the shoulder-tapping portion of the ceremony.

Thus, from the beginning, an "accolade" suggested praise for accomplishment. But for several hundred years, it referred to the specific ceremony, which contained detailed actions—including the ceremonial embrace that formed the word in the first place.

As knighthood became more of a spectacle (Sir Mick Jagger, anyone?), and knights of old became fodder for the novels of Sir Walter Scott, the word "accolade" lost its connection to a specific ceremony and became instead a generic word for "praise."

Of course, if you've done something really good for your significant other (unexpected flowers, breakfast in bed, etc.), then your accolade may still include an embrace around the neck.

A

---

accost

ORIGINAL DEFINITION: to come up to the side of (focusing on the action of ships)
NEW DEFINITION: to challenge aggressively

When you hear the word "accost," you might picture pushy salespeople, debt collectors, pissed-off landlords, or an angry spouse taking you to task for leaving the toilet seat up (again!!). Chances are, you don't picture boats, but at one time, you would have.

The word "accost" contains the same root as the word "coast" because, initially, the word referred to actions that ships took during battles—or potential skirmishes—at sea. For example, a ship would come up alongside another boat to see if the other ship contained friends or foes. Or, a ship would approach the coastline and threaten a town.

The word also had the milder, non-nautical definition of addressing someone formally, but you will probably encounter this version of "accost" solely in English novels of manners. In addition, Shakespeare occasionally used the word "accost" to mean simply "approach" . . . minus the aggression.

As piracy and naval battles became less common—though both still occur today, of course—the word "accost" became more generic. It still suggests someone approaching you aggressively, but he or she doesn't have to be in a boat in order to put you on the defensive.

A

—— *Trix Are for Women* ——

Men who accost the women in their lives by leaving the toilet seat up, farting at will, and believing that picking up after themselves is "women's work" will meet their match if the "little woman" turns into an agitatrix. This rarely used word means "female agitator." She's the type who won't accept Neanderthal behavior from her mate. She'll push right back.

Whenever you see "trix" at the end of a word, it denotes the "feminine" version of a better-known word. Here are some others you've probably never heard:

- administratrix: female administrator
- creatrix: female creator
- fornicatrix: female fornicator
- imitatrix: female imitator
- janitrix: female janitor
- oratrix: female orator
- victrix: female conqueror (female form of victor)

acorn

ORIGINAL DEFINITION: generic nut
NEW DEFINITION: "nut" from an oak tree

If you want to say somebody's crazy, you might say he's "nuts." Once upon a time, you could simply have said he was an "acorn." Prior to the sixteenth century, "acorn" was generic for nut.

In Old English, "acorn" had a slightly different spelling, and its roots contained a word meaning "fruit." Just as people once called pinecones pineapples (see entry for "pineapple") because they are the "fruit" of a pine tree, folks called nuts "fruits" since they are the "fruit" of various trees.

From the Old English and well into the Middle English period of our language, an "acorn" was the generic word given to the "fruits" of the forest trees, from which farm animals gained sustenance.

By the sixteenth century, "acorn" came to be associated exclusively with the oak tree because the mighty oak was the king of feeding swine. It's comparable to the way some modern trademarks have become synonyms for various products. For example, Band-Aid is a generic term for an adhesive bandage and Kleenex refers to facial tissue.

The various root spellings of "acorn" were "akarn" or "akram," but since the Old English word for "oak" was "ac" and the object was used like "corn" to feed the animals, the spelling of the word shifted to the present-day "acorn."

acquit

ORIGINAL DEFINITION: to pay off a debt
NEW DEFINITION: to declare innocent or not guilty in a court of law

Long before "acquit" became part of an oh-so-ripe-for-punning piece of courtroom doggerel, it had a different, though related, meaning.

In the early thirteenth century, "acquit" meant to satisfy a debt or claim. For example, let's say your neighbor loaned you twenty-five guinea fowl, and you repaid him a year later with thirty-five geese. You had "acquitted" your debt. The word carried with it the sense that something had been done. You had to actively do something to cause the debt in the first place, then do something to pay it off.

A

By the late fourteenth century, "acquit" began to suggest that no debt or claim rightfully existed to begin with. People associated it with wiping out a debt or claim, so they emphasized the fact that the debt was gone. By the seventeenth century, the word was dragged into the courts in the form of "acquitted," which meant that, though you had been accused of bearing responsibility for some action or debt, a jury found that you were not, in fact, responsible for it.

The late defense attorney Johnnie Cochran breathed new life into this stale legal term by making it part of an immortal couplet during the O. J. Simpson murder trial: "If it doesn't fit, you must acquit."

acre

ORIGINAL DEFINITION: open, tillable land
NEW DEFINITION: a unit of measure equal to 43,560 square feet

Originally, an acre meant open space that a team of yoked oxen could till in one day. For several hundred years, an acre had no specific measurement. Thus, the Old English word "acre" meant almost any expanse of arable land.

Yet some oxen clearly covered more land than others. As time went on, and people began to want ownership quantified, the acre measurement became more standardized. By the tail end of the Middle Ages, an acre was equal to about 40 rods × 4 rods (a rod measuring 16.5 feet). You do the math.

By the time people started homesteading in the western United States, an acre was equal to its current measure of 43,560 feet, which is just a little smaller than a football field. Who knows what people of old would have thought of today's "zero-lot-line" homes.

—— *God's Acre* ——

To this day, some church graveyards are referred to as "God's acre" because they are "sown" with the bodies of believers. The expression is a modern embodiment of "acre's" original meaning, "field," and has nothing to do with the modern measurement.

A

actual

ORIGINAL DEFINITION: active
NEW DEFINITION: real; existing in fact

"Actual" was once a vital, action-packed word. It was a mover and shaker. Over time, thanks to the French language, it became a couch potato.

Originally, "actual" was to acts as "factual" is to facts or "natural" is to nature. Something factual has to do with facts, and something natural has at least a tenuous relationship with nature. Something actual was something active.

In the thirteenth and fourteenth centuries, you might have spoken of an "actual" plow horse, meaning one used on a regular basis. Or you might have had an "actual," on-the-side relationship with thy neighbor's wife, which meant you were, um, visiting her regularly.

English is a mutt, however, so before long, an old French word ("les actualités") with a similar construction got intermingled with "actual." The French word meant "news"—as in, the report of a fact. This commingling is the likely reason "actual" stopped being active and became passive.

Thus, something actual now means something already accomplished, something real, something factual that exists. It's "old news."

adamant

ORIGINAL DEFINITION: mythical, unbreakable stone
NEW DEFINITION: dogged in maintaining a position

Scientists of the Middle Ages believed in a mythical mineral that was unbreakable. They called it adamant. If found, they believed it would have been useful for any number of purposes: defense, construction, prisons, etc.

Various minerals and hard materials were called "adamant" in medieval times, including white sapphires, magnets, and steel. Ultimately, most associated the mythical adamant with real diamonds.

Once the identity of adamant was settled, people began to use the word metaphorically. As a noun, "adamant" meant an unbreakable stone, so when people transformed it into an adjective, "adamant" meant hard, unbreakable, unconquerable, and invincible. Thus, the adjectival form of "adamant" has had a wider scope than the noun form.

By the nineteenth century, "adamant" began to take on a mostly negative connotation. Pundits and wags commonly referred to people whose ideas—some might say whose heads—were hard and unbreakable as being "adamant."

To this day, "adamant's" synonyms are a stubborn bunch, including such hardheaded words as: headstrong, truculent, mulish, tenacious, inflexible, obstinate, and recalcitrant.

addict

ORIGINAL DEFINITION: to deliver over to, as a slave (verb)
NEW DEFINITION: one who is dependent on narcotics; one who is dependent on anything (noun)

When you hear the word "addict," you are likely to think of B-list celebrities who, once again, are taking up residence for "exhaustion" in some tony rehab center. But "addict" didn't become associated with narcotics—nor did it become a noun—until the dawn of the twentieth century.

For more than 2,000 years, "addict" was a verb with many dark meanings: to sacrifice (as in, on an altar, not as in doing something selfless for others), sell out, betray, give over. Most definitions suggested slavery or enslavement in some way. You would "addict"—or sell into slavery—someone whom you bested in battle, for example.

Thus, the path from ancient "addict" to modern "addict" traces a smooth metaphorical groove. To "addict" was to enslave someone. An addict is someone enslaved to narcotics. After that connection was made around 1900, the newly minted noun eventually went on to describe people "enslaved" to everything from pornography to television to video games.

addle

ORIGINAL DEFINITION: urine; filth
NEW DEFINITION: to confuse; mix up

What does "addle" have to do with rotten eggs? Quite a bit, actually

The Old English word from which "addle" derives meant urine or liquid filth. Eew, gross. In the 1100s, you might have walked into your house and stepped in addle left by your dog or your small child.

By the thirteenth century, a connection was made between liquid filth and rotten eggs, likely because both are gross things that smell bad. A common expression of the day was "addle egg," which meant hen fruit (eggs) that had become putrid. Folks in medieval times didn't exactly follow today's food pyramid religiously, but even they knew to avoid addled eggs.

By the 1600s, "addle" changed meaning and parts of speech. The noun became an adjective describing anything putrid, not just eggs. Then, the word broadened even more. First, it designated something useless, which makes sense. Urine is a waste product, after all.

Finally, thanks in part to seventeenth-century poet and critic John Dryden, "addle" began to take on its modern meaning of "confuse" or, more specifically, the adjectival form of the word, "addled," which means confused or mixed-up.

Dryden is credited with coining the expression "addlepated," which he intended to mean, "a head filled with unsound, mixed-up, putrid ideas."

---

aftermath

ORIGINAL DEFINITION: second growth of grass, after the first growth has been harvested

NEW DEFINITION: that which follows; often associated with disasters

Originally, in the sixteenth century, "aftermath" was farmer jargon for a second growth of grass. The first crop, harvested for feed and grain or hay, was gone. If the season stretched into the

A

fall, a second growth of grass popped up. Thus it was "after" the "math," which was an updated version of an Old English word for "mowing."

By the seventeenth century, "aftermath" extended metaphorically to mean "that which follows," just as the original meaning described the patch of grass that sprang up after the first had been harvested. It was a neutral word and technically still is, though its association with man-made and natural-made disasters (see entry for "disaster") has given it a seamy reputation.

"Aftermath" is one of those words that, today, has a negative connotation because it's so often used by reporters to describe the chaos following a disaster. For example, Jane Smith of Channel 2 News will explain how, "The aftermath of the hurricane left dozens dead and caused millions of dollars of damage." By contrast, you don't usually hear about the "aftermath" of a delightful picnic or an enjoyable day in the country.

—— *The Aftermath of Discordianism* ——

Discordianism is a satirical "religion" created in the 1950s. The focus of its worship is Eris (a.k.a. Discordia), the goddess of chaos. Disciples of Discordianism believe that order and disorder are artificial states. There is only reality. In this respect, the "faith" is a lot like Zen Buddhism. This religion even has its own calendar, which contains seventy-three-day months: Chaos, Discord, Confusion, Bureaucracy, and The Aftermath. The Aftermath, as its name suggests, is "a time of cleaning up the mess."

album

ORIGINAL DEFINITION: white
NEW DEFINITION: book of keepsakes; phonograph record

The Beatles released an album in 1968 called *The Beatles* but known to most as "The White Album" because of its stark white cover, containing only the words "The Beatles" on it. Did they, or did most record buyers, know that there actually was a connection between "white" and "album"?

In ancient Rome, "albus" meant "white" and "blank." Romans used the name to denote the tablet on which public notices were posted because, prior to any postings, the tablet was both white and blank. Before long, people began using the word "album" to mean the collection of notices themselves, ignoring the word's "white" roots.

As the word was adopted into English, people emphasized the concept of pictures or items placed on pages. Albums became books of photos or autographs or various odds and ends. But the sense of "white" lingered.

In the twentieth century, people began to use "album" to describe phonograph records, and this meaning actually harks back to the word's original denotation. Records usually had inner, protective sleeves that were blank and stark white.

allude

ORIGINAL DEFINITION: to mock; make fun of
NEW DEFINITION: to make an indirect reference

At one time, "allusion" and "ludicrous" were kissin' cousins. If you "alluded" someone, you made fun of her. Maybe you mocked the mannerisms of your teacher, for example. "Ludicrous" also suggested a similar play or sport (see entry for "ludicrous").

Just how did "allusion" stop meaning "mock" and come to be a concept that continues to stymie high school English students?

A lesser meaning of "allude" was "to play with," and an allusion does "play with" language as well as create a puzzle for the listener or reader to figure out. If someone says, for example, that a couple seems like Romeo and Juliet, then she could be saying the couple exemplifies true love . . . or that it's hopelessly doomed.

Another key to the change is in the mocking itself. People in the early sixteenth century "alluded" someone by aping his mannerisms. In so doing, they were "alluding" to that person, in the modern sense of the word, by making an indirect reference to him.

---

amazing

ORIGINAL DEFINITION: terrible, dreadful
NEW DEFINITION: really wonderful; causing amazement

When "amazing" first began to be written in the fifteenth century, it meant something akin to the modern sense of "causing amazement" or "stupefying" you. If God were to come down from the sky and stand next to you in a cornfield, that would have been amazing then, just as it would be amazing now.

However, by the 1700s, something "amazing" meant something that would fill you with wonder. The word took on a pejorative connotation and referred to something dreadful. You found your best friend in bed with your wife? Amazing. The king is going to tax you even more? Amazing.

A

This sense of the word was a metaphorical leap from "stupefying." If something makes you feel stupid or insensible, then it must be bad, right? By the turn of the eighteenth century, however, "amazing" shifted again and often described something "wonderful."

Thus, "amazing," like many contemporary politicians, could be accused of being a "flip-flopper."

—— *Amazing Grace* ——

John Newton was your quintessential bad boy. A sailor who participated in the eighteenth-century slave trade, Newton loved to make up profane ditties to pass the time. One night, his ship was caught in a dreadful storm. Newton's fear of the terrible storm led him to call out to God for mercy, also known as grace.

Newton survived the storm and transformed his life. He was ordained by the Church of England in 1764, and in 1773, he wrote a poem to accompany a sermon. The poem was called "Amazing Grace," and it was autobiographical. He was the "wretch" who had been "saved." In 1835, "Amazing Grace" was joined to an extant tune and became the staple of Sunday morning services it continues to be today.

---

ambulance

ORIGINAL DEFINITION: mobile or field hospital
NEW DEFINITION: conveyance for getting someone to a standing hospital

If you've seen the movie or television show *M*A*S*H*, then you've seen an ambulance. No, not those trucks that bring patients to Hawkeye and the gang. The field hospital itself was the ambulance. It brought the care to you . . . not the other way around.

A

Look at the word. It has the same root as words like "ambulatory" or "amble." In essence, the word means "walking." The French term from which the English derives was "hôpital ambulant," but English dropped "hôpital." The bottom line is that the emphasis was on walking, on movement.

Then came the Crimean War (1853–1856). Sometimes considered the first "modern" war, this struggle for control of the former Ottoman Empire was the first to use railroads and telegraphs tactically.

In addition to giving literature (and dismayed students) Lord Tennyson's "The Charge of the Light Brigade," the Crimean War was when people began to refer to ambulances as the conveyances moving troops from the field to places where their injuries were treated.

The change likely occurred because the war had so many different theaters. Field hospitals couldn't possibly have kept up with all of the battles. Thus, ambulances took you *to* the hospital instead of *being* the hospital. Field hospitals still exist today, of course, but they're no longer called ambulances.

---

amuse

ORIGINAL DEFINITION: to delude; deceive
NEW DEFINITION: to appeal to one's sense of humor

From the Middle Ages into the eighteenth century, "amused" had a mostly negative connotation. It was used to describe someone diverting your attention while trying to cheat you. For example, a minister who preached fire and brimstone to cover up the fact that he was breaking multiple commandments would have been described as "amusing." (Actually, some might still find him amusing.)

As early as the mid-1600s, the word was occasionally used the way it is today. It described something preoccupying, especially something humorously preoccupying; something that puzzles or bewilders you. Nonetheless, it continued to be a synonym for "deception" and "trickery" for another hundred years. Now, however, it has dropped its deceptive tone and simply means something humorous.

Amuse vs. Bemuse

Good news! You're not the only one who gets the definitions for "amuse" and "bemuse" mixed up. Nowadays, if something bemuses you, then it puzzles or bewilders you. At one time, something or someone "amusing" did the same thing—but now, "amuse" usually refers to something humorous. So the next time someone corrects you for using the wrong word, you can explain why you are not as bemused as you may seem. So . . . are you bemused yet?

---

apron

ORIGINAL DEFINITION: from "napron," meaning napkin or tablecloth
NEW DEFINITION: garment worn over one's clothing to protect from spills and other household messes

"Apron" comes, via Latin, from an Old French (the Gallic version of Old English) word "naperon," changed ultimately in English to "napron." The Latin word meant napkin, and the French word meant tablecloth.

The shift in the word's denotation was complete by the 1600s. Tablecloths protect tables from food and drink spills. Napkins clean stains off of your face. Thus, it wasn't too great a leap to make "napron" gain its current meaning. Aprons, after all, are like tablecloths for your body.

But why is the word "apron" instead of "napron"?

English is a great hodgepodge, and when it was newly minted, confusion reached Babel-like proportions. For example, the French pronunciation (and difference in the articles used with nouns) made "un naperon" sound like "un aperon." Thus, a lot of folks thought people were saying "an apron" rather than "a napron."

And that's how we got a seemingly boring word that shouldn't exist at all. Umpire (see entry for "umpire") is another example of this French to English screw-up.

---

artifice

ORIGINAL DEFINITION: workmanship demonstrating craft or skill
NEW DEFINITION: trickery; deception

"Artifice" is a word that can be said to have an infancy, an adolescence, and an adulthood.

As an infant, "artifice" suggested cunning or skill. Note that word "cunning." When *that* word was born around the fifteenth century, it contained seeds of "artifice's" contemporary meaning. Thus, "artifice" was not always a positive word.

As an adolescent, however, "artifice" shifted until it did have a completely positive connotation. If a builder of tables showed "artifice," it meant he or she showed great skill and craftsmanship

A

Presumably, someone who told good stories showed "artifice" as well.

When "artifice" grew up, it once again took on the mostly negative connotation it contains today. One reason is that the word, as noted, once contained the sense of "cunning." If someone is cunning, then he's probably being tricky. Granted, he may be using his wits to help out humanity, but most of the time, cunning suggests someone trying to get away with something.

In addition, the word suffered from its association with "artificial." Originally, "artificial" was a neutral word, used simply to differentiate goods made by humans from goods "created" by nature. However, "artificial" came to have the pejorative taint it contains to this day, and "artifice" suffered as a result.

---

assassin

ORIGINAL MEANING: hashish user

NEW MEANING: one who commits murder for political reasons

What does John Wilkes Booth have to do with hash? Oddly enough, there is a connection.

In 1090, a Muslim religious leader named Hasan ibn al-Sabbah created a fiefdom near Tehran. He surrounded himself with fanatical followers and came to be known as "The Old Man of the Mountain."

Hasan and his followers struck terror in the hearts of many. They had no problem killing political enemies because they believed they, themselves, were doing the work of God. If one of Hasan's followers was killed during an attempt to murder enemies, they believed he would go straight to heaven. Some modern terrorists have the same belief today.

Hasan and his followers also were known to smoke hashish. The visions the drug gave them were supposed to be glimpses of the heaven that awaited them upon a martyr's death. Therefore, followers of Hasan were called "hashishyy," which, through the vagaries of English pronunciation, became "assassin."

Hasan and his successors continued killing political opponents until the Mongols came along and unseated them in the thirteenth century. Although he has been gone for a thousand years, Hasan's evil legacy of politically motivated murders continues straight on to John Wilkes Booth and Lee Harvey Oswald.

Lesser-Known American Assassins

Four U.S. presidents have been assassinated, but Charles Guiteau and Leon Czolgosz are not exactly household names.

Guiteau assassinated James Garfield just four months after Garfield's inauguration. Guiteau, a one-time member of the utopian Oneida Community, had delusions of grandeur. He believed he should be appointed to a cushy governmental sinecure and was upset that Garfield didn't agree. Guiteau shot Garfield on July 2, 1881, in a Washington D.C. train station. Garfield lived two months after the shooting. Ironically, the bullet didn't kill him. His doctors did, because antiseptic medicine was still a couple of decades away in the United States.

Michigan-born Czolgosz became enraptured by anarchistic beliefs. As a result, he decided to assassinate President William McKinley, believing it would help the United States . . . somehow. McKinley was in Buffalo visiting the Pan-American Exposition when he was shot by Czolgosz on September 6, 1901. Even improved medicine couldn't save McKinley, who died from his injuries on September 14.

attic

A

ORIGINAL DEFINITION: pertaining to Athens (usually capitalized)
NEW DEFINITION: top story of a home, usually filled with junk

Greece may be floundering in debt at present, but hundreds
of years before the birth of Christ, it was the very cradle of culture. Athens, in particular, was the site of cultural advancements
unmatched since.

Athens sat on the Greek peninsula of Attica, and since Athens
dominated the peninsula, "Attic" became an adjective and was
used interchangeably with the word Athenian. Amazing advancements in philosophy, poetry, athletics, and architecture—among
others—characterized the "Attic way."

Now, jump in a time machine and move ahead to the eighteenth century. Even though Athens was no longer a cultural
mecca, "Attic" architecture still represented a sophisticated, cos-
mopolitan, and educated class of people. Thus, businesses and
institutions began to build structures in an "Attic" style. In fact,
that style still is used today.

Peaked roofs, placed over the main structure, were the part of
a building that seemed most "Attic." Thus, for a time, "attic" (with
a small "a") meant "decorative façade above a building's main
story." Ultimately, attic became the word to describe the room
behind that façade and, nowadays, is associated primarily with private homes, rather than with public structures.

The condition of most modern attics—junk filling every corner, rats, mice, spider webs—would likely give the average Athenian of old a coronary.

awful

ORIGINAL DEFINITION: worthy of respect or fear; inspiring awe
NEW DEFINITION: abhorrent, offensive

A

Picture yourself hundreds of years ago, seated at a friend's table. She's just provided you with a meal. As you eat the food, you shake your head contentedly and say, "Gee, this is awful!" It would have been a compliment.

The word "awful" first appears in the fourteenth century, and it suggested something or someone who filled one with terror . . . God, an angel, a divine being. The Bible is filled with the word. In Hebrews 10:31, for example, the anonymous writer tells his readers, "It is an awful thing to fall into the hands of the living God."

Obviously, the scribe was not saying "it's a terrible thing." He was saying, "It's a scary but awe-inspiring thing." After all, he was exhorting his readers to stand up strong in the face of persecution. Later, "awful" suggested anything that inspired awe . . . such as an excellently prepared meal, for example.

By the nineteenth century, "awful" became mainly pejorative. Something inspiring awe or dread simply became "something that's pretty darn bad." A bit later in the 1800s, the word gained another use and became equivalent to the adverb "exceedingly," as in "awfully nice to see you."

backfire

ORIGINAL DEFINITION: fire set ahead of a larger fire, to deprive the larger fire of oxygen
NEW DEFINITION: to achieve the opposite—and probably negative—result of a planned action

B

"Backfire" originated in mid-nineteenth-century America. Firefighters realized that they could stop large fires by setting small fires behind them, thus robbing the larger fires of oxygen and snuffing them out. When the internal combustion engine was born, the concept of backfire was borrowed to describe the sound made when an engine doesn't "fire" properly.

At some point, the word also began to be used to describe the action of certain firearms that would kick back toward one's body when fired. All of these various uses of "backfire" existed simultaneously by the early twentieth century.

Ultimately, the word gained a metaphorical use at least loosely associated with all of its earlier meanings. Not every firefighting backfire worked; sometimes the process just caused additional damage. Engines that don't fire properly can ruin your plans. Guns that hurt you instead of an intended target produce the opposite of your desired effect.

Firefighters may still speak of a backfire because the process is still used, but for most, "backfire" refers to plans that blow up in your face . . . an appropriately fire-themed expression.

backlog

ORIGINAL DEFINITION: a large log at the back of a fireplace
NEW DEFINITION: tasks that have piled up

Do you think that modern Americans invented the art of ignoring work . . . especially during the holiday season? Well, think again. Europeans of the mid-seventeenth century perfected this art long before online solitaire or Angry Birds existed.

During the Christmas season, the man of the house would go into the woods and search for a really thick log. He would take it home, put it toward the back of the fireplace, build a good-sized fire, and let that sucker burn.

Since it was an extremely large log—called a yule log in honor of the season—it took a very long time to burn. The custom was that, as long as the yule log was burning, he could blow off work and most daily tasks. Of course, that meant the work piled up. But so what? He would drink another nog and forget about it!

Eventually, the log succumbed to ash, and it was back to work . . . and all those tasks he had ignored. By the nineteenth century, "backlog" came to refer to all those accumulated duties. What would those folks of the seventeenth century have given for the onscreen yule log cable companies offer at Christmastime? No more work again ever . . . until your cable gets shut off for nonpayment.

baffle

ORIGINAL DEFINITION: to disgrace publicly
NEW DEFINITION: to bewilder; confuse

"Baffle's" transition in meaning is, appropriately, baffling . . . in the modern sense.

Initially, the word was used to describe, say, a knight who had demonstrated cowardice or been found guilty of perjury or some other crime. After being found guilty, he had "baffled" himself.

By the mid-seventeenth century, "baffle" lost that meaning and became the familiar word we know today. But why?

Here's one clue: In the eighteenth century, sailors wrote of "baffling" winds, which meant winds that blew from various directions and "confused" their ship. Then, in the mid-nineteenth century, "baffle's" other current meaning came into being: something that drowns out light or noise.

But neither of these changes fully explains the transition. Most likely, the word changed due to the incredulous responses elicited by stories of those who had been disgraced. If a lord or lady found out that a gallant knight was stealing swine, then he or she would have been shocked, surprised, confused, and bewildered by the news. Good people doing bad things? Baffling!

---

balderdash

ORIGINAL DEFINITION: drink comprised of a mix of liquors
NEW DEFINITION: nonsense; drivel

Nowadays, greedy barkeeps water down their drinks, while charging you full price. During Elizabethan times, bartenders had a different way to save some money.

Let's say the pub owner was running low on several things: wine, beer, hard cider, etc. He sure didn't want all that stuff to go to waste, so he mixed it all together. The resultant concoction was called "balderdash," though it's not clear if this was its "official" name or an insulting name given to it by customers.

Come to think of it, the customers probably didn't care. Most likely, the bartender would sell this swill, which often—gag—included milk, cheaply. Thus, everyone was happy. Bartender gets rid of the crap at the bottom of the bottle or keg; customer gets cheap intoxication.

The word "balderdash" derives from a Danish word meaning "clatter," as in "confusing noise." Thus, it's easy to see how "balderdash" stopped referring to cheap booze and, by the mid-seventeenth century, meant someone speaking (or writing) nonsense. If your meaning is all jumbled up, then, metaphorically, it resembles that stuff you drink when you're looking to get drunk but your coin purse is nearly empty.

B

—— *Balderdash = Bullsh*t!* ——

"Balderdash" is a colorful word that now makes a nice euphemism for the word "bullshit." Early American movie actors were kings and queens of euphemism, in part because the movies were for so long forced to avoid swear words. (Even certain seemingly innocuous words couldn't be said under any context: virgin, nuts, goose, and madam, among them.) Here are some of the more creative ways Americans in Hollywood sidestepped a curse word:

- W. C. Fields would sometimes say "Godfrey Daniels" when confronting something annoying, irritating, or absurd. The nonsense name was simply a way to avoid saying, "Goddamn."
- The Marx Brothers could be heard to say, "Jumping butterballs." God only knows what that took the place of.
- Humphrey Bogart couldn't even pause when asking Dooley Wilson, "what the . . . are you playing" as Wilson began to play "As Time Goes By" in *Casablanca*. Viewers might insert the word "hell."

bandwagon

ORIGINAL DEFINITION: circus wagon carrying a band
NEW DEFINITION: a movement, often political, with a lot of support

At first, "bandwagon" meant exactly what its name suggests: a wagon with a band on it. Picture a bunch of excited children, watching as the circus rolls into town on a Saturday morning. The procession would head toward an open field, in which rings and tents soon appeared like magic. Somewhere in the midst of the parade was an open-air wagon on which a band played to drum up excitement, as though any additional prodding was necessary.

From the 1850s until the early 1900s, that's what a bandwagon was. Nowadays, however, no one pictures a wagon with a band on it if someone says, "Looks like you've joined the bandwagon" . . . unless maybe he attended clown college. So how did the word's scope expand to politics?

Since circuses often took time off during the year, those wagons had downtime. Politicians, always eager to get publicity cheaply, found good use for the bandwagons during the circus's "off-season." Since they contained built-in excitement, politicians put their own musicians on one of those wagons, had the band strike up "For He's a Jolly Good Fellow," parade through town, and got everyone thrilled about their campaigns. Thus, the association between politics—or anything else that people consider important, like sports or fashion—and "bandwagons" was born.

barbarian

ORIGINAL DEFINITION: foreigner
NEW DEFINITION: person considered backward and inferior

B

Believe it or not, "barbarian" was not always a negative word. Because ancient Greece once was the indisputable cradle of culture, Greeks considered "foreign" anyone who didn't speak Greek. To the Greeks' ears, foreign languages sounded like babble, like people just making nonsense syllables such as "bar, bar, bar." Thus, they called these foreigners "barbaroi," which later became "barbarian" in English.

That's why "barbarians," for centuries, just referred to foreigners. The word didn't have an explicitly negative connotation. However, human beings haven't changed all that much over the centuries. A tendency to think of foreigners as somehow mentally deficient, physically awkward, or just plain bad because they're "different" always has been an unfortunate human trait.

That unbecoming trait is why the word "barbarian" no longer necessarily suggests foreigners, but it does suggest people who are not as sophisticated, educated, or capable as people in the middle or upper classes. Today, "barbarian" is also an insult many women use to describe the men in their lives when they act uncivilized, backward, and uncouth. It's better than some other words they could use to describe the men in their lives.

—— *Famous Conans* ——

Until the arrival of late-night talk show host Conan O'Brien, the most famous Conan was a barbarian, a character created in 1932 by Robert E. Howard.

basket case

ORIGINAL DEFINITION: quadriplegic
NEW DEFINITION: someone unable to cope emotionally

Unlike many of the words in this book, whose meanings shifted centuries ago, "basket case" is a term that developed and subsequently changed meaning fewer than 100 years ago.

Initially, "basket case" was coined in England to describe soldiers left quadriplegics on the battlefields of World War I. Since these men either literally had lost their limbs or had lost the use of them, the men were sometimes carried around in baskets.

Even if they weren't actually carried around in baskets, the term became a common way to describe people with this plight. "Basket case" likely was an example of the kind of gallows humor that people, such as doctors or police officers, develop to cope with the horrors of their professions.

"Basket" also suggested that these soldiers would be unable to work once they returned to their former lives. The world was not designed for "differently abled" people to work or live happily, so most quadriplegics would be forced to carry "baskets" and beg for money.

The insensitivity of the term "basket case" led to its disappearance as a quadriplegic descriptor, but at some point in the second half of the twentieth century, the meaning of the term shifted to a metaphorically disabled person . . . but is still insensitive.

Now, it suggests someone who doesn't have the use of his or her *emotional* faculties, due to stress, overwork, or relationship problems. In effect, these folks suffer from a feeling of hopelessness not unlike that which is felt by someone who's lost the use of his or her limbs.

bathroom

ORIGINAL DEFINITION: room equipped with a bathtub
NEW DEFINITION: room equipped with a toilet

The word "bathroom" began to appear in writing by the end of the 1700s. At that time, its meaning was quite literal. The bathroom was a room with a bathtub.

B

The timeline makes sense if one compares it to the history of the flushing toilet. Sure, those wily Greeks invented a primitive flush toilet for King Minos of Crete some 800 years before the birth of Christ. The Romans invented sewers and had outhouses. Queen Elizabeth had a flush toilet, invented for her by her godson.

But it wasn't until the mid-1800s that indoor plumbing became "de rigeur." By that time, a word that had emphasized bathing became a word that referred to a room with a toilet. Bathtubs, or the lack of one, became less important than the presence of a toilet because, after all, it was gross and gauche to mention unmentionable (though very necessary) toileting activities. Thus, by the early 1900s, the word became almost strictly a euphemism for "place to go relieve oneself."

—— *Unmentionable Activities* ——

Bathroom and restroom are the main words used to denote "place that includes a toilet." At various times, that place also has been called a privy chamber, a necessary room, the smallest room in the house, and even "where the queen goes alone."

Even in the twenty-first century, some blanch at the prospect of mentioning the porcelain throne. So, it's no surprise that English has amassed tons of euphemisms for the activities that actually go on in the bathroom.

For "poop," the squeamish have or have had the following: pick a daisy, pluck a rose, bury a Quaker, go to the prayer house, go to the thinking place, spend a penny, do one's duty, and—during World War II—go call on Hitler.

For "pee," consider the following: shake the dew off the lily, shake hands with my wife's best friend, water the roses, and make room for another beer.

B

belfry

ORIGINAL DEFINITION: siege tower (slightly different spelling)
NEW DEFINITION: bell tower, often connected to a church

Now associated with churches (and people who have "bats" in theirs), "belfry" once was a word of war.

During the mid-to-late Middle Ages, a belfry was a moveable siege tower. At that point, it was spelled "berfrey" or "berfrei." Troops would bring their catapults and clubs and spears onto the battlefield, while some poor grunts pushed the "berfry" along. Some lucky soldiers in the tower could keep a lookout for the enemy and shoot medieval missiles at them from their lofty perch.

By the mid-1400s, "berfrey" began to refer to watchtowers in general. Someone keeping watch over a town stood in a "berfry" and looked for signs of trouble. When he saw them, he needed something with which to warn everyone of possible danger. Thus, bells were introduced to "berfries." At that point, thanks to the bells, the word shifted to "belfry."

Initially, "belfry" suggested a tower not attached specifically to another building. Think, for example, of St. Mark's Campanile, the famous belfry that stands in Venice's Piazza San Marco. Completed in 1514, it's a classic example of the "stand-alone" belfry. Nowadays, most bell towers are simply part of a church building itself.

B

bidet

ORIGINAL DEFINITION: a small horse
NEW DEFINITION: a low-lying basin used to clean one's most intimate areas

In the 1600s, you might have taken your paramour for a ride on your "bidet." After all, a small horse is just right for romance, since it forces its riders into close proximity.

The word transformed due to a metonymic shift. Metonymy is a form of figurative language in which one substitutes a name for one thing with something closely related to it. For example, athletes are "jocks" because male athletes wear jockstraps. Big-business tycoons are "suits" because they wear them. The kettle doesn't actually boil, but the water inside it does . . . and so on.

Expand the concept a bit, and ponder the position one might take when riding a small horse. It's the same basic position one might use with the newly defined version of a bidet. As the eighteenth century progressed, the bidet lost its equine associations entirely.

Nowadays, the last thing you'd associate with a bidet is romance.

bimbo

ORIGINAL DEFINITION: slang for a stupid, inconsequential man
NEW DEFINITION: slang for a stupid woman with loose morals and large physical assets

"Bimbo" is a shortened form of the Italian word "bambino" (baby) and was used to demean men. For example, someone being "unmanly" might have been called a "bimbo" as an insult.

Since "baby" has been a term of endearment for one's (typically female) lover as early as the mid-nineteenth century and "bimbo" was short for the Italian word for baby, it wasn't much of a stretch to transform male "bimbos" into female "bimbos." If a male "bimbo" was a man not acting like a man was supposed to act, well then, a female "bimbo" was a woman not acting like a woman was supposed to act.

The word was used extensively during the Jazz Age of the 1920s. After all, that's when women started bobbing their hair, wearing scandalously short skirts that exposed ankles, and dancing the Charleston on tabletops after imbibing bathtub gin. In short, they weren't acting ladylike!

The word was moribund for most of the rest of the twentieth century, until sexual scandals involving politicians became the infotainment events they remain today. Suddenly, it seemed, all manner of presidents, presidential hopefuls, and televangelists were squiring bimbos on the side.

The word caught on once again, and it's still going strong. Ironically, in light of its "male" origin, the word "himbo" was coined in the 1980s to describe male bimbos.

blank

ORIGINAL DEFINITION: type of coin; white; shining
NEW DEFINITION: unfilled space

For a word that basically means "nothing," as in no writing, a spot where a picture used to be on a wall, or an empty stare, "blank" has had—and continues to have—a pretty fulfilling life.

B

Most of "blank's" root words are akin to "white" or "shining." That's one reason a common coin during the reign of Henry V was called a "blank." It was really shiny. It also wasn't worth much, so "blank" and "worthless" began a relationship.

For a time, during the sixteenth century, the most common meaning of the word "blank" was the white space at the center of a target. The center of the target was white, but it was also empty until filled by arrows. Thus, a connection between "blank" and "empty" was formed.

Also during that century, losing lottery tickets were called blanks, which gave rise to the still-extant expression, "to draw a blank." Again, there was a connection made between "blank" and "nothing" since a losing lottery ticket is worth nothing.

By the nineteenth century, "blank" started to be used in place of dirty words, e.g., "You son of a blank." Not long after, it was used—without the word "cartridge"—to describe a harmless bullet. Perhaps the connection is to a blank stare that one sometimes associates with soldiers who have been too long in battle.

From all these associations—empty, worthless, nothing— comes the current-day meaning of "blank."

bleak

ORIGINAL DEFINITION: pale
NEW DEFINITION: hopeless; depressing

At one time, something "bleak" was simply pale. "Bleak" derives from older words that developed into the word "bleach." Therefore, someone's tunic might be "bleak" from being out in the sun, or someone's face would be "bleak" from not getting enough sun.

By the early 1700s, the word made a metaphoric shift. If something was "bleak," meaning "pale," then it had been used up or abused or drained of its liveliness. Thus, something "bleak" became something hopeless and depressing, something drained of vitality.

Bleak House, Charles Dickens's tenth novel, captures well the transition of the word. The novel focuses on a court case that drags on for years, allowing the property at the case's center to become a slum, thus making it both "paler" and increasingly hopeless for its denizens.

--- *Bleak Fish* ---

Unless you know that "bleak" once meant "pale," you will probably wonder why a common species of fish is known as a bleak.

The common bleak is a small-mouthed, pointy-headed fish that, while sometimes eaten, typically is used as a bait fish. The fish are, as "bleak" once suggested, very pale and opalescent. In fact, when they're not being used to catch larger game fish, a bleak's scales often are used to make artificial pearls.

bless

ORIGINAL DEFINITION: to mark with blood
NEW DEFINITION: to praise; glorify

The roots of this word all suggest blood, as in the type one might spill sacrificially on an altar. This meaning of "bless" endured through the Old English period. In effect, "bless" is left over from pagan rituals, during which one would give thanks to a god or some gods by slaughtering animals and leaving their blood on an altar. Of course, such rituals are found throughout the Old Testament as well. Remember, for example, that Abraham was able to substitute a goat for his beloved son Isaac when God asked for a sacrifice.

As Christianity took over the West, "bless" changed in meaning. Christians no longer believed in the validity of blood sacrifices, save that of Christ himself, so "bless" developed an image problem. By the Middle English period, "bless" kept the meaning of "to give thanks and praise" but lost the need for animal slaughter and blood spills.

Somewhere along the way, "bless" also took on another meaning. In addition to praise and glorify, "bless" also means "confer happiness upon." There's no reason, based on "bless's" history, that this should be one of its meanings. It's due to a semantic mistake. Folks just got "bless" and "bliss" mixed up.

---

bohemian

ORIGINAL DEFINITION: gypsy
NEW DEFINITION: nonconformist writers and artists

The French word "bohémian" meant "gypsy," and "gypsy" comes from a Latin word meaning Egyptian. Yet the meanings of both of these terms—gypsy and bohemian—are wrong. The Romans

B

wrongly believed the gypsies were from Egypt, and the French wrongly believed they were from Bohemia.

Bohemia, which no longer exists, was in central Europe. It occupied what is now the western two-thirds of the Czech Republic. These "bohemians," as the word became in English, were itinerants. They had no permanent home, and many looked down on them. Some believed they dabbled in magic, and others thought they were intrinsically dirty. Still others thought they were charlatans (see entry for "charlatan") who made their living selling worthless elixirs.

The word changed thanks largely to the author William Makepeace Thackeray (1811–1863). His most famous novel, *Vanity Fair*, featured a protagonist named Amelia Sedley, and her foil, Becky Sharp.

Sharp is described as being the daughter of parents who were "bohemians" by choice. Sharp herself is an actress, singer, and musician. The popularity of the novel—and of Sharp—transformed "bohemian" from a gypsy to an artistic person who lives, like a gypsy, outside of mainstream society. For that matter, "gypsy" now has less to do with ethnicity—as far as most are concerned—than it does with someone who is a free spirit. Essentially, "gypsy" and "bohemian" now are synonymous.

boulevard

ORIGINAL DEFINITION: top of a military rampart
NEW DEFINITION: broad thoroughfare

"Boulevard" comes from the same root as "bulwark," and the root words mean "tree trunk" and "work." The idea was that the defensive ramparts, or walls, of a town were built of tree trunks, and, obviously, it took a lot of work to get all those trunks lined up in proper protective positions.

When a village no longer needed its "boulevards," they often would be torn down and replaced with flat streets. The French continued to call these routes "boulevards."

The width of paths that once were city walls was much greater than the width of the average city street. Thus, "boulevard" came to refer to any particularly broad street, especially if it was decorated with trees. Given that "boulevards" once were trees, this seems appropriate.

Nowadays, "boulevard" is, for most people, synonymous with street, lane, way, drive, etc. It's just a generic word for street that city planners sometimes choose because it sounds romantic. Boulevards aren't necessarily wider than any other throughway.

B

---

bravery

ORIGINAL DEFINITION: boasting; defiance (negative connotation)
NEW DEFINITION: courage (positive connotation)

The words from which "bravery" originates aren't positive. Italian and Spanish words suggest rashness, akin to "bravado," while an earlier Latin word carries with it the sense of someone not "brave" but "barbarous."

Thus, "bravery" used to carry with it a suggestion of daring . . . but in a pejorative sense. If one were "brave," then one was probably foolhardy in the face of danger. He or she was the kind who would attack even when seriously outnumbered.

By the late sixteenth century, "bravery" began to transform into a laudable quality. It became a compliment, rather than an insult. By this time, most likely, even rash acts of courage were considered manly and reflected well on a king's leadership.

The word's original meaning is still reflected in a less-common use of the word "bravery." In addition to "courage," "bravery" also refers to fine clothing, the kind one might boast about or show off in.

B broadcast

ORIGINAL DEFINITION: act of scattering seed
NEW DEFINITION: transmission of a radio or television program

Many of the words in this book changed meaning as Middle English transformed into Modern English, but "broadcast" is one that owes its most common current meaning to an important modern invention: radio.

When everyone farmed, a "broadcast" was a scattering of seed. Picture serfs out on huge, craggy landscapes throwing out handfuls of seed for their lords and ladies, dreaming of the day they might have a little land of their own.

Long before the advent of modern broadcasting, the word "broadcast" took on a figurative meaning. As early as the late eighteenth century, the word was used to describe anything being spread: news, disease, new inventions, etc. It's no coincidence that the word shifted at this time, during which the industrial revolution was in full swing and the Western world was becoming less agrarian.

When radio became the, um, television or Internet of its day, "broadcast" was used figuratively to describe the programs that were "scattered" to the masses. Thus, by the 1920s, "broadcast" had almost nothing to do with agrarian seeds and everything to do with urban radio transmissions. When television became king, "broadcast" transferred to that medium as well.

—— *The First Star of Broadcasting* ——

Most fans of the boob tube have never heard of Stooky Bill, but they wouldn't be enjoying the latest product-pushing "reality" series if it weren't for this guy, who was a real dummy.

Scottish television pioneer John Logie Baird produced what many consider the first television broadcast in 1925. He successfully took an image in one room of his apartment and broadcast it into another room of the apartment.

Baird's technology required very hot lights, which made it impossible for a human subject to be the first "television star." That honor, instead, went to Stooky Bill, the head of a mannequin. "Stooky" is a type of plaster of Paris.

Baird broadcast Stooky Bill's visage, but at quite a price to the dummy, who now sits in England's National Media Museum (formerly the National Museum of Photography, Film, and Television). Due to the hot lights, Bill's hair is singed, his face is cracked, and his lips are chipped.

B

broker

ORIGINAL DEFINITION: wine cask opener
NEW DEFINITION: mediator between buyer and seller

In long-ago France, a "brokiere" was one who tapped kegs and opened wine casks. A prestigious job it wasn't, but don't tell that to today's snooty, snarky sommeliers! The word "broach," as in "broach the subject," comes from the same root. If you broach a subject, you open it up for consideration. The lowly wine broacher developed into the slightly tonier wine merchant.

Fourteenth-century English folk borrowed the word "broker" and used it—sometimes with the word "love" in front of it—as a euphemism for pimp. A "love broker" opened up negotiations between a john and a soiled dove.

Ultimately, "broker" became a generic term for "middleman," someone who negotiates between buyers and sellers. Nowadays, "broker" calls most immediately to mind a "stockbroker." Those who blame Wall Street for the nation's various economic crises may be pleased to know of the connection between brokers and pimps.

B

brothel

ORIGINAL DEFINITION: vile person of either gender; later, a prostitute
NEW DEFINITION: a place where one procures prostitutes

Men of Chaucer's day may have insulted other men by calling them "brothels." They weren't suggesting that these men frequented whorehouses. At that time, either men or women could be "brothels": foul, vile, worthless individuals falling into ruin who could drag you down with them. The word was akin to something like "big jerk."

Before the Middle Ages had even ended, "brothel" became associated exclusively with women. After all, women in those days were "ruined" if they "soiled themselves" before marriage, so prostitutes were referred to as "brothels." Where did "brothels" ply their trade? In brothel-houses, of course.

By the time Shakespeare began writing plays, a metonymic shift had occurred. Metonymy substitutes one thing for something else closely related to it: "Suits" are powerful businesspeople, "crowns" are kings, etc. Thus, "brothels" stopped being people and became the buildings in which those people, um, worked.

browse

ORIGINAL DEFINITION: to feed on buds
NEW DEFINITION: to skim; look casually

Poetic types may speak of cows "browsing" in a pasture, which means they're looking for yummy stuff on which to nosh. For some 400 or so years, that's all "browse" meant. It had a pastoral tinge.

B

"Browse" currently brings to mind walking through a bookstore, scanning the titles at the Redbox, looking through matches at an online dating site, or using a web "browser." Yet, the modern sense of "browse" didn't really come into common use until midway through the nineteenth century.

The metaphorical connection between the old and new definitions isn't difficult to make. Farm animals "browsing" in a pasture are flitting about, seeking good buds, and simply passing by with a glance anything that doesn't suit their fancy.

Change cows and goats to men and women, plop them down in front of a Vegas buffet, and they'll do the very same thing: look casually, search for the just-right morsels, and ignore anything that seems unappetizing.

buccaneer

ORIGINAL DEFINITION: user of a "boucan"
NEW DEFINITION: a pirate

What? You don't know what a "boucan" is? It was a primitive version of today's barbecue grill, used by West Indian natives. What do "boucans" have to do with pirates?

Indigenous West Indians used "boucans" to smoke oxen over a fire. They were among the first of the world's peoples to have the equivalent of backyard barbecues. Then the English, Dutch, and French invaded the West Indies in the seventeenth and eighteenth centuries. This was the "golden age" of Caribbean piracy, as glorified by Walt Disney World and Johnny Depp films.

It's the French whom the English language has to thank for "buccaneer." The French quickly borrowed the natives' habit of roasting meat on "boucans." Thus, they began to be referred to as "boucaniers," or "those who use 'boucans.'"

The word passed into English as "buccaneers." Since most of the French busy using "boucans" were pirates, "buccaneer" became synonymous with freebooters.

---

buffoon

ORIGINAL DEFINITION: pantomime dance
NEW DEFINITION: a clown; a fool; a simple-minded person

Mimes, fairly or unfairly, tend to be among the most denigrated of performers. Plug the words "everyone hates a mime" into Google, and you'll get over 70,000 results. YouTube has plentiful videos carrying the same theme. You may wonder—if you ever wonder about mimes—if there was a time when mimes were loved and adored. Well, no, not since ancient times.

Originally, a "buffoon" basically was a mime, and some people (the French?) may have found him amusing. He (you know it must have been a "he") would prance around, act silly, and puff out his cheeks. The last part is important because "buffoon" derives from a word meaning "to puff out one's cheeks."

Somewhere between the mid-sixteenth century and today, "buffoon" was used to describe anyone who acted foolish. The "puffing cheeks" no longer were as important as the fact that a "buffoon" was—and is—someone who doesn't have much of sub-stance to say and who acts simple-minded, despite (presumably) having normal intelligence.

—— Everybody Loves a Mime ——

Mimes were never a big hit . . . except, as it turns out, in ancient Rome. The Latin word "pantomimus" means "imitator of everything." Using simple masks, body language, and dance, a "pantomime" would silently act out all the characters of a tragedy.

Did you catch that? A tragedy. That's one of the main differences between a "pantomime" and a just-plain "mime." Pantomimes were figures of tragedy, while mimes typically are figures of farcical comedy. Pantomimes made you cry. Mimes make you laugh.

The "pantomimus" first "took off" during the reign of Augustus (63 B.C.E.–14 C.E.) and remained popular until the Roman Empire fell. Since that time, most people have indeed hated mimes (and pantomimes too, for that matter).

B

bugger

ORIGINAL DEFINITION: heretic

NEW DEFINITION: derogatory slang for one who engages in sex acts some consider unnatural; performing such acts

For most people, the Greek Orthodox Church is the place that has the annual festival with all the yummy desserts. The rest of the year, no one (who isn't Greek Orthodox) gives it much thought. Is it Catholic? Is it Protestant? Who knows? Pass the baklava!

The church is in fact part of Eastern Orthodox Christianity, which is very similar to Roman Catholicism. But don't say that, even today, to members of either church. These faiths are close to the same age but differ on such key issues as marriage for priests (okay in Eastern Orthodox, as long as he was married before ordination; a no-no in Catholicism) and the Immaculate Conception of Mary (Catholics say yea; Eastern Orthodox says nay). For Protestants and folks who sleep in on Sunday, these matters seem like mere quibbles.

B

What does this have to do with "buggers" and "buggery," you ask? Plenty, as it turns out.

Roman Catholicism felt that members of the Eastern Orthodox Church were heretics. One sect Catholics hated most practiced their faith in Bulgaria. Thus "buggers," as these Bulgarians came to be known, were heretics.

Since the Catholics didn't like them anyway, they decided these "buggers" weren't just heretics. By the 1500s, Catholics believed they engaged in sexual practices that included anal sex between same-sex partners and the deflowering of farm animals. It was really just a case of vilifying competitors.

This derogatory notion of "buggers"—sparked by religious feuds—gave rise to the modern sense of "bugger" and its related term, "buggery."

---

bully

ORIGINAL DEFINITION: sweetheart
NEW DEFINITION: one who threatens or harms others without cause

Talk about a change of heart! Initially, "bully" was a positive word. It came from roots that meant lover or brother (as in, friend . . . you know, "What's happening, brother?"). Thus, either gender might make goo-goo eyes and call one another "bully." This would have been done until the early 1500s.

At least two theories abound that suggest why "bullies" gained their negative reputation. One possibility is the resemblance of "bully" to "bull," a word that took on metaphorical meanings: stubborn, nonsense, large, etc.

The other theory is juicier. At one time, "bully" was a synonym for "pimp." Perhaps it was used sarcastically, perhaps not. The problem with this theory is that "bully" already had come to mean "guy who beats you up on the playground because he outweighs you by fifty pounds" before the first recorded use of "bully" as a synonym for "pimp." It may have been used verbally before it appeared in writing, however.

B

—— *Theodore Roosevelt's Bullying?* ——

Fans of Theodore Roosevelt may recall that "bully" was a favorite word of the twenty-sixth president. He was using it in the earlier, more positive sense. He also coined the term "bully pulpit."

For Roosevelt, the presidency is a sweetheart of a place to espouse one's favorite causes. As a result, he referred to it as a "bully pulpit." Since his time, however, people have forgotten there ever was a positive meaning of bully—and pulpit, for most people, has religious overtones. At one time, a pulpit was simply a generic word for a platform.

buxom

ORIGINAL DEFINITION: humble, obedient
NEW DEFINITION: full-bosomed

Most contemporary men would like the buxom women of today to be like the buxom women of old. Originally, the word meant humble, obedient, compliant. In today's parlance: easy.

The word first began to appear in the middle of the Middle Ages, and it referred to humble and obedient young women. In fact, "buxom" stems from an Old English word meaning, ahem, "capable of being bent." Adolescent minds among you, please put an appropriate joke here.

Gradually, "buxom" began to shift in meaning. The word was applied to lively, healthy young ladies. At a time when many people were starving, "healthy" often meant, well, plump. Picture the paintings of Rubens, who was born in 1577, at the dawn of the modern era.

As fashions and tastes have continued to change, "buxom" has become less associated with "plump" and more associated with "voluptuous" (yes, men are pigs). Less Rubenesque, more like the woman described in The Commodores's "Brick House."

C

cabal

ORIGINAL DEFINITION: mystical interpretation of the Old Testament, sometimes spelled with a "k"

NEW DEFINITION: shadowy group meeting in secret, often for nefarious purposes

The original meaning of "cabal" is closely related to the Kabbalah. It was simply a mystical interpretation of the Hebrew Bible, as opposed to practical interpretations dealing with one's day-to-day behavior. Remember the 1990s, when the Kabbalah became the "mystical philosophy du jour" of celebrities like Madonna? Basically, the Kabbalah is the mystical branch of Judaism that describes the connection between God and human beings.

The key point is that, from the beginning, the word "cabal" suggested something mysterious and secret. That meaning was solidified, and turned explicitly pejorative, during the reign of England's King Charles II.

Charles's reign was controversial, and so was he. He seems to have left illegitimate children in every village of England, and he ruled during the Great Plague, which killed about 100,000 people. In addition, he had some shady guys working for him: Sir Thomas Clifford, Lord Arlington, Duke of Buckingham, Lord Ashley, and Lord Lauderdale.

This group, whose initials were CABAL, spent most of its time concerned with infighting, rather than on strengthening ties between England and France, as it was exhorted to do. Folklore suggests that Charles II's group was largely responsible for giving cabals their bad name.

carol

ORIGINAL DEFINITION: a type of dance, not necessarily religious
NEW DEFINITION: a type of song, associated with Christmas

One popular pastime of the early Middle Ages was "caroling," or dancing in a circle to songs written in Latin. Yep, those peasants really knew how to have fun, didn't they?

Almost from the beginning, the word "carol" referred to both the dances and to their accompanying songs. In their earliest incarnation, "carols" could be religious—but they didn't have to be. Sometimes these dances, and their songs, were written and performed for festivals, some of which were pagan.

Sometimes, however, "carols" were used to accompany so-called mystery plays. A mystery play wasn't so much a full play as a scene of a Christian miracle, performed to music (though, in time, they became more like "real" plays). For example, the resurrection of Christ would have been a typical mystery play. Over time, "carol" came to have an exclusively religious connotation and lost its "pagan" roots.

Why are most carols "Christmas carols"? During the Protestant Reformation, many eschewed such nonessential church trappings as carols. They practically ceased to exist. When they staged a comeback in the late 1500s to early 1600s, many of the earliest were written for Christmas.

C

censor

ORIGINAL DEFINITION: census taker
NEW DEFINITION: one who removes objectionable content from a film, book, etc.

While the ancient Greeks were busy inventing philosophy, fine architecture, theater, and all sorts of other cultural advancements, the ancient Romans tried to do the same. Overall, they weren't as successful. Even today, they seem like the "also-rans" in the ancient cultural wars.

C

Romans always seemed to have a more practical bent. They were right-brained. They perfected useful inventions, such as aqueducts (though, these actually had already been developed initially by the Greeks and several other cultures), and they excelled at government.

Even today, most (except the elected leaders in Washington, apparently) understand that governments require revenue. No one likes taxes, but almost everyone realizes they're a necessary evil in order to keep a nation or republic strong. The ancient Romans were nothing if not great tax collectors.

In order to make an accurate assessment of taxes, the Romans started taking a census. If they knew how many people were in a community and what sorts of possessions they had, then they could squeeze from them the maximum amount of taxes.

A "censor" was someone tasked with collecting census data. He learned about more than what folks owned, however. Sometimes, he would report immoral behavior he witnessed. Thus, he became associated with upholding public morals.

Over time, censor has lost its connection to the census and to taxes. Nowadays, a censor is someone whose job is to uphold the morals of a given society by ridding media of content some consider immoral or objectionable.

charisma

ORIGINAL DEFINITION: a gift from God/the gods
NEW DEFINITION: personal magnetism

Although the modern sense of the word "charisma" has existed since the 1920s, the word might as well have been invented for the thirty-fifth U.S. president, John F. Kennedy. He radiated health, humor, and vig-ah (vigor). He seemed to live a charmed life . . . until Camelot came crumbling down, that is.

Kennedy's personal magnetism certainly played a factor in his triumph over his dowdy, frowning, not-made-for-television rival, Richard Nixon. The gods seemed to have favored Kennedy.

Using that example, it's easy to see the connection between the new and old versions of "charisma." Originally, the word referred to gifts bestowed by the gods or by God, and it came to refer to the "gift" of a person's exceptional personal attributes. Initially, someone with "charisma" was believed favored by Jehovah himself.

Most likely, he or she had a talent for leadership, for bending others to his or her will. This ability, still so magical when one experiences it, truly does seem to be divinely bestowed.

The original sense of the word is retained in "charismatic" churches, in which people are said to demonstrate the divine gifts of healing, speaking in tongues, and handling serpents.

charlatan

ORIGINAL DEFINITION: indulgence peddler
NEW DEFINITION: malicious, money-grubbing trickster

Indulgence peddlers were the used car salesmen of medieval times. The Roman Catholic Church, which *was* the Christian

Church in most of Europe, sometimes ran short of cash. When that happened, they sold indulgences. Basically, these were "get-out-of-hell-free" cards. For the right price, you could buy an indulgence that would remove pretty much any sin.

Indulgence peddlers had to use the same high-pressure tactics as the modern-day car salesman in order to bilk money from their clients. Of course, they had the added benefit of being able to, literally, scare the hell out of people. In Italy, indulgence peddlers were called "cerretanos" after the community of Cerreto, which was notable for its indulgence peddlers. In English, the word ultimately became "charlatan."

In the sixteenth century, the Church stopped selling indulgences. "Charlatan" then became a word primarily used to describe those who claimed to sell "medicine" that could cure all manner of evils. Like indulgence peddlers, they sold objects of dubious value using high-pressure sales tactics.

Eventually, "charlatan" became connected to any huckster, swindler, mountebank, con man, and phony, from those selling cars with rolled-back odometers to those who sell the Brooklyn Bridge to foreign tourists.

clown

ORIGINAL DEFINITION: peasant; someone from the country
NEW DEFINITION: circus performer

"Clown" is a word like villain (see entry for "villain") for which the English language has snobbery to thank. Associated today with circuses and children's nightmares, "clowns" once referred to people who lived out in the country.

For example, if you've read Shakespeare, you'll find his works are populated with "clowns." When you first encountered the Bard in high school, you might have pictured . . . well, clowns, in makeup, with bulbous, oversized shoes. After all, Shakespeare's "clowns" did offer what passed in those days for comic relief. In fact, the "joke" was that "clowns" were people from the sticks, and therefore backward, compared to urbane city dwellers like Shakespeare (who actually came from the sticks himself but clearly forgot where he came from—shame on you, Bill!).

Even as Shakespeare was still writing, "clown" began to mean something akin to what it means today. The country-bumpkin version of a "clown" got mixed in with some of the "clowns" of Italian theater, who wore makeup and outlandish costumes.

Ultimately, "clowns" became staples of traveling circuses, known for pantomime, fright wigs, and fitting en masse into tiny cars.

C

—— *Coulrophobia?* ——

Psychologists—and many children and adults—agree that a morbid fear of clowns exists. Yet etymologists don't agree on whether the word "coulrophobia" is "real" or a pseudointellectual coinage of recent origin. What's coulrophobia? The name for the morbid fear of clowns.

"Phobia" means fear, of course. Some etymologists believe that the first part of the clown-fearing word has its origins in an ancient Greek word that means, basically, stilt-walker. After all, some clowns do walk around on stilts.

Other logophiles suggest "coulrophobia" relates to the modern Greek word, "klooun," which means "clown." And still others believe the word is just supposed to look like it came from one of these legitimate origins but was, instead, created out of whole cloth, possibly as a joke

complexion

ORIGINAL DEFINITION: bodily constitution; personality
NEW DEFINITION: appearance or color of facial skin

Back in medieval medicine, people believed in "the four humors," and the amount of each in your body determined your overall personality and constitution:

1. An excess of black bile made you a depressed person.
2. Too much yellow bile made you intrinsically a grouch.
3. A lot of blood made you a party animal.
4. And excess phlegm made you, well, phlegmatic, or calm.

In addition to affecting your personality, these humors also affected your physical health. Sad people were considered sickly, for example. The word "complexion" originally had to do with someone's combination of humors.

How could medieval physicians determine one's "complexion"? The best way, in their estimation, was to look at the color of someone's face. For example, even though the color scheme eludes us today, a red-faced person clearly had too much yellow bile to an ancient physician. Someone overly pale probably didn't have enough blood. And so on.

Humorism—the name for the "science" of humors—eventually gave way to modern medicine, but it took a while. Vestiges remained into the eighteenth century, when "bleeding" someone was a common way to treat a sick patient. The belief remained that too many fluids could build up in the body, and doctors could bleed out the bad fluids. Though humors stopped taking any part in medical diagnoses, the concept of "complexion" as one's facial appearance or color remained.

computer

ORIGINAL DEFINITION: one who calculates
NEW DEFINITION: programmable electronic device

Sure, someone who performs calculations or computations by hand could still be called a "computer," but for most of the twentieth century and beyond, a "computer" refers to an electronic device that seems to have frighteningly little need of puny humans.

The word "computer" has existed since the mid-1600s. For the first 250 years of its existence, a "computer" was a person who calculated sums by hand. He or she would be not unlike a modern-day accountant.

"Computer" first began to refer more to machines than to human beings just before the turn of the twentieth century. In 1886, for example, William Seward Burroughs (grandfather of the Beat Generation writer of the same name) began to mass produce the adding machine he invented. Some folks called it a "computer" because . . . well, that's what it did. It computed sums.

The first "modern" computer was ENIAC, Electronic Numerical Integrator and Computer, developed in 1946. It officially associated machines and computers. ENIAC took up an entire floor of a building.

When microprocessors appeared in the 1970s, home computers began to emerge. By that time, computers—like science-fiction cyborgs—had completed their transformation from human to machine.

C

confused

ORIGINAL DEFINITION: defeated; beaten (as in battle)
NEW DEFINITION: chaotic; muddled

Appropriately enough, "confused" has a confusing history. Originally, it was used interchangeably with "confound," which once meant to mix or mingle a bunch of things together. A party would be "confounded" or "confused." Stew would be "confused" and "confounded."

C

Eventually, "confused" took on a military air. It was a word used if one side was routed in a battle. You can picture men, horses, servants, all running around in disarray. Thus, the seed for connecting "confused" with "chaos" and "muddle" was forged.

But before that became common parlance, "confused" was more akin to "embarrass." If a group of knights or soldiers has to retreat, then the combatants who survived probably were embarrassed. Ultimately, this meaning remains, but it's not as common as "chaotic." Geoffrey Chaucer seems to have used "confused" in a way similar to how it's used today, which may ultimately have helped the word gain its present, most prominent meaning.

Finally, "confused" is confused because it existed as an adjective before it gave rise to the verb "confuse," which didn't become a common word until the mid-sixteenth century. Usually, the verb comes first, followed by an adjective formed from it.

cope

ORIGINAL DEFINITION: to fight with; strike (as a blow)
NEW DEFINITION: to deal effectively with a difficult situation

Talk about a 180. From roughly the 1300s to the 1600s, "cope" was a belligerent verb that suggested striking or fighting an enemy.

You might "cope" somebody on a field of battle, or "cope" them because they were messing around with your wife.

By the middle of the seventeenth century, however, the word evolved to mean "handle a situation." One likely reason for the change is that this type of "cope" was influenced by another, less-well-known meaning of "cope": an ecclesiastical garment. It's the kind that completely covers someone. Poets have borrowed this meaning to describe the "cope of night" or the "cope of someone's heart." Thus, a "cope" covers up something. Some might say that is one way to handle a difficult situation.

Another way to handle a difficult situation is to confront it head-on, to fight with it or to strike it, metaphorically speaking. If you beat the crap out of someone, then you've dealt with the situation (just not in the most effective way). Thus, "cope" may have changed meaning because fisticuffs and drastic actions were (and are) used often to deal with tough times and difficult people.

C

---

courage

ORIGINAL DEFINITION: feelings; temper
NEW DEFINITION: bravery

The Cowardly Lion wanted courage so much that he braved a difficult trip to the Emerald City in order to find it. Once there, however, he discovered he had possessed courage all along. He acted, despite his fear, which is the very definition of "courage."

But it wasn't always.

Initially, "courage" was a more generic word. It summed up all manner of one's innermost feelings. The word was like a synonym for "mood." Thus, your "courage" could be bravery, but it also could be fear, anger, lust, greed, pride, or any other of the seven deadly sins.

Somewhere along the way, "courage" came to refer principally to "bravery." Most likely, that's because the root word of "courage" is the Latin word for "heart." The expression "take heart," meaning "find courage in the midst of a difficult situation," has existed for centuries.

C

—— *Quotable Courage* ——

- "We must build dikes of courage to hold back the flood of fear." –Martin Luther King Jr.
- "All our dreams can come true if we have the courage to pursue them." –Walt Disney
- "Courage is what it takes to stand up and speak; courage is also what it takes to sit down and listen." –Winston Churchill
- "Courage is not simply one of the virtues, but the form of every virtue at the testing point." –C.S. Lewis
- "Courage is being scared to death . . . and saddling up anyway." –John Wayne
- "Whatta they got that I ain't got? Courage." –The Cowardly Lion (as played by Bert Lahr in *The Wizard of Oz*)

crass

ORIGINAL DEFINITION: solid; thick
NEW DEFINITION: crude

You probably know someone who's a little dense. She doesn't seem to realize when she's overstepped the bounds of polite society. She makes crude remarks in mixed company. Her colleagues might call her (among other things) "thickheaded."

The metaphorical "thickness" of someone's head is how the word "crass" switched meaning from "solid" or "dense" to "crude" or "coarse."

During the 1500s, you might make a "crass" stew or even live in a "crass" building. The word simply suggested sturdiness. By the 1650s, "crass" began to refer almost exclusively to people who should not be allowed to mingle in mixed company because they were thickheaded, rude, or crude.

The word also got tainted by snobbery. The "cradle-rich" disdain parvenus, those who came into "new money" in what the rich think is "the wrong way." The truly rich—sniff, sniff—don't need to *display* their wealth. Thus, the always-wealthy described self-made people as crass.

C

---

craze

ORIGINAL DEFINITION: to break; shatter (verb)
NEW DEFINITION: fad (noun); to derange (verb)

Before the sixteenth century, something that was "crazed" was completely shattered or ground into tiny shards. Another meaning for "craze" (which actually remains today, though it's obscure) was "to cause cracks in." For example, in pottery, you may intentionally "craze" your creation for aesthetic reasons.

By the sixteenth century, "craze" lost its original meaning and was used mostly to describe a breakdown in physical health. This first metaphorical shift makes sense because, when your health is gone, you're pretty much shattered.

Not long after "craze" defined physical weakening, it was used to describe mental breakdowns as well. Thus, "craze" began to mean "derange" or "make crazy."

"Craze" underwent one more shift in the nineteenth century when it began to be used as a word for "fad" as in, "It's the dance craze that's sweeping the nation!" A fad is a form of temporary mania, and "craze" is a synonym for "mania"; thus, the connection is made.

crisscross

ORIGINAL DEFINITION: Christ's cross
NEW DEFINITION: pattern of crossed lines

C

Beginning in the fifteenth century, generations of children learned the alphabet using something called a hornbook. The letters in hornbooks were carved on wood or stone, which was then covered with a thin veneer of mica (a type of common rock) or animal horn (hence the name) for protection.

The top line of the alphabet page in a hornbook typically began with a large cross, followed by various letters. The cross was a symbol of luck. To begin lessons, teachers would say something like, "Please start at the Christ's cross row." Then, students would trace their fingers back and forth over the lines and learn the alphabet, spelling, or new vocabulary.

Over time, "Christ's cross row" became the contraction "crisscross row" and ultimately just "crisscross." The act of reading, which causes one's eyes to move in a, well, crisscross manner, led to the word developing its present meaning. Nowadays, most don't have a clue that there's a religious origin to "crisscross."

culture

ORIGINAL DEFINITION: the tilling of land
NEW DEFINITION: arts and customs that particularize a group, society, nation, etc.

Centuries ago, the word "culture" referred specifically to tilling land; it was related to the word "cultivate" (which, incidentally, also has transformed metaphorically to mean more than just growing plants and flowers).

Metaphor also explains the transformation of the most common contemporary meaning of "culture." At first, around 1500, the word was used to describe the result of a good education. Matriculation into a school led to a "culture" of the mind.

Centuries later, the word transformed to something akin to "high culture," the sort of stuff you might learn in school: poetry, symphonies, operas, etc. The rise of so-called "low culture" (comic books, tabloids, B-movies, etc.) helped make "culture" what it is today: the good, the bad, and the ugly of any given society, office, nation, or group.

Nowadays, you read about "corporate culture," that collection of potential land mines that you can trip when you get a new job. Or, you study the culture of the Far East. Or you talk about how so many young people today eschew culture altogether.

C

C

—— *Low Culture TKOs High Culture* ——

In 1962, Andy Warhol shocked the art world by producing a silk-screen canvas that's come to be known as *Campbell's Soup Cans*. Although so-called pop art already existed, Warhol's work was the shot heard 'round the art world.

Abstract expressionists and the high-art aficionados who bought abstract expressionist works abhorred Warhol. Abstract expressionism is nonrepresentational and, for most, just looks like a bunch of paint rubbed or dripped onto a canvas. Arguably, the most famous painter of this school is Jackson Pollock.

On the other side of this cultural divide were artists like Warhol and the everyday folks who absorbed popular culture like a sponge. They decided that advertisements, comic books, and popular products deserved to be considered high art. They won, as evidenced by the proliferation of "artsy" advertisements strewn throughout the typical high-brow magazine like *Vanity Fair*.

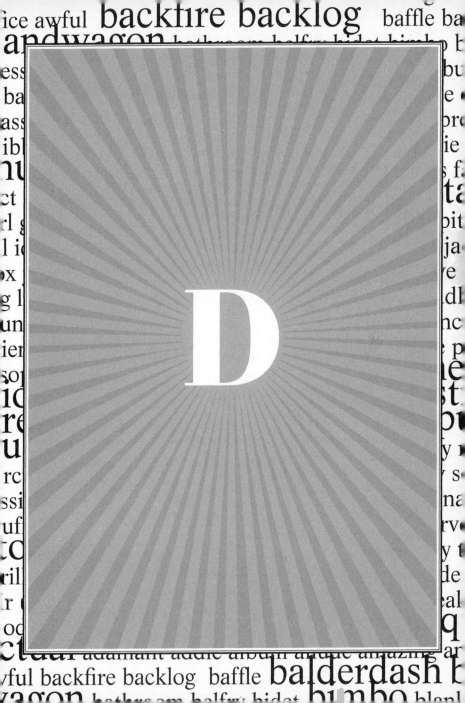

dab

ORIGINAL DEFINITION: to strike with a weapon
NEW DEFINITION: to press lightly and repetitively

From the 1300s to the 1550s, "dab" meant "to strike a heavy blow with a weapon." Picture knights of old with those spike-covered clubs going at on one another for the courtly love of a fair maiden.

And then "dab" became less brutal. The rise of firearms contributed to the word losing its power. People weren't as likely to club each other with weapons; they shot each other instead.

D

More importantly, the mongrelization of English came into play: Many confused "dab" with the Old French word "dauber," which led to the English word "daub" (meaning to smear or coat something). Thus, some painters were said to "daub" paint onto their canvases . . . sometimes as a compliment and sometimes as an insult. By the 1600s, "dab" developed its modern meaning, paving the way for cheesy radio and television jingles promoting hair products.

---

daft

ORIGINAL DEFINITION: gentle
NEW DEFINITION: simple-minded

Believe it or not, this word didn't start out as an insult. Its Old English version actually suggested someone gentle. By the Middle Ages, it began to refer to someone who was dull. The transition, in part, was due to the fact that many gentle people are perceived as, well, dull. They don't do exciting things. They don't start fights or play rugby.

In addition, "daft" is a good example of the muddle caused by the great English word "salad." "Daft" became akin to "feeble-minded" because the word resembled "daffe," which meant "half-wit."

Fans of British comedy are familiar with this word in its current form, which is used the way Americans throw around "moron," "idiot," and "imbecile" (see entries for "idiot," "imbecile" and "moron"). If you're doing something others perceive as stupid, then you're "daft." For example, if you "drink and dial" your ex-girlfriend, then your British buddies will call you "daft" (or worse).

<hr>

D

decimate

ORIGINAL DEFINITION: to kill one in ten
NEW DEFINITION: to destroy almost completely

"Decimate" is a word logophiles love to hate because they claim that—sniff, sniff—almost everybody uses it improperly.

Initially, "decimate" was used to describe taking one-tenth of something. During the classical period, it became associated with a particular military action. If a legion—a large group of soldiers—was found to be guilty of cowardice or mutiny, then one out of every ten men in that legion would be slaughtered in recompense. Thus, "decimate" would lead to a relatively small number of executions, all things considered.

Technically, "to decimate" is still to reduce by one-tenth. The problem is that people got confused somewhere in the seventeenth century. Most likely, while some understood the "correct" meaning of "decimate," others believed it meant to reduce something *to* one-tenth of its former size, rather than just *taking away* one-tenth.

If that's confusing, think of it this way. You have a hundred soldiers. If you "decimate" this group, you have ninety soldiers. If you reduce the group to one-tenth of its former size, however, then you only have ten soldiers remaining.

That's a big discrepancy, yet the confusion caused by it remains to this day. That's why it now means to destroy something almost completely.

---

deer

D

ORIGINAL DEFINITION: animal; beast (generic)
NEW DEFINITION: specific animal

Supposedly, the Inuit (i.e., Eskimos) have dozens of words for snow. They see more of the white stuff than anything else, so it makes sense. Likewise, some Indian tribes are said to have dozens of words for corn because corn is so central to their lives and culture.

Popularity—or omnipresence—of a thing explains how "deer" transformed from a generic word for "animal" and became, well, Bambi's mother.

An Old English word for animal was "deor," or deer. The word was used for any creature other than a human being, though the word usually was restricted to wild animals. Even before Old English shifted to Middle English, "deer" began to restrict itself to the denizen of today's petting zoos.

One likely reason is the popularity of hunting deer. You can imagine how confusing it must have been if you were hunting deer, specifically, and people kept asking you, "Yeah, but what *kind* of deer?" meaning, "What kind of animal?" So people started to call a deer a deer and move on.

---

defecate

ORIGINAL DEFINITION: to purify; cleanse
NEW DEFINITION: to poop

"Ah," someone might have said circa 1570. "It smells so nice in here. Someone must have defecated!"

At that time, the word suggested purification, cleaning, getting rid of clutter. "Defecation" comes from a Latin word meaning to purify or cleanse from the dregs—dregs being the last little bit of liquid in a container, the stuff that's probably 90 percent backwash. Getting rid of that stuff left your wineskins much more sanitary.

By the middle of the nineteenth century, the word began to take on its main present-day meaning: to have a bowel movement. Those refined Victorians needed polite ways to discuss horrid bodily functions, and besides, bowel movements "purify" the body and rid us of the "dregs" of last night's repast.

It's likely those same Victorians would have fainted dead away if they'd known a term their earthier Old English ancestors used for defecation: arse-gang, or "ass going."

D

> —— *What a Crock!* ——
>
> In the early 2000s, the Internet became filled with, well, shit. Various bloggers and pseudointellectuals claimed they had found the origin of this common—and vulgar—word for defecation.
>
> The alleged origin story goes something like this: Some ships had the misfortune to carry manure across the high seas. When the manure was stored below decks, water would get into the ship, causing fermentation to begin. As the manure fermented, it released methane gas. Inevitably, someone would go to the hold, light a cigarette, and KABOOM! Sailors finally determined the problem and realized the manure had to be stored above the water line. Thus, they would write on their cargo paperwork the acronym S.H.I.T., which meant "Ship High In Transit."
>
> The story is a crock. In fact, the word "shit" has been around since at least the 1400s, and its roots are Old English via German, Danish, and Swedish words, all of which always meant "dung."

D

derrick

ORIGINAL DEFINITION: hangman
NEW DEFINITION: device for lifting large objects

Thomas Derrick was accused of rape and pardoned by the Earl of Essex on one condition: Derrick had to agree to be an executioner. Elizabethan times weren't that different from today. Who wants to admit their job title is executioner?

Derrick was very good at his job, which began in 1601. He hanged more than 3,000 people during his career, including— irony of ironies—the Earl of Essex, his erstwhile pardoner. Derrick was so associated with executions during the Elizabethan era that his name became synonymous with hangman.

During his tenure as executioner, Derrick also became a tinkerer (see entry for "tinker"). He made improvements to the gallows, such as adding a pulley system. Prior to Derrick's enhancements, hangmen just threw the rope over the top of the gallows beam. Derrick made hanging more efficient and more likely to result in a quick death.

Derrick again lent his name to his profession. People began to call his gallows a "derrick." The modern sense of "derrick" comes from the fact that a derrick looks a lot like a gallows and often works with a pulley system similar to the one Thomas Derrick devised.

deprecate

ORIGINAL DEFINITION: to pray against something, in order to make it go away
NEW DEFINITION: to put down; belittle

D

"Deprecate's" roots explicitly contain an entreaty to pray. But let's face it, if you're praying *against* something, then, clearly, you don't approve of it. You think it is worthy of disparagement. That's how the term came to refer to putting something down, or belittling it.

Today, you often hear the term within the phrase "self-deprecating." Most folks like self-deprecating people because they don't seem to take themselves too seriously. One understands that someone putting herself down doesn't really mean it; she's just trying not to sound too full of herself when, for example, she makes a wise point during an argument.

disaster

ORIGINAL DEFINITION: unfavorable arrangement of stars
NEW DEFINITION: sudden, chaotic event

Ronald Reagan famously believed in the stars. He had an in-house astrologer who may or may not have influenced the fortieth president's policy decisions. And, of course, some people can't go a day without consulting their horoscopes. Few scholars today consider it a legitimate science, however.

At one time, astrology was a universally accepted science. Intellectuals and the rabble alike believed that the position of stars and planets guided the destinies of individuals and cultures. For proof, consider the fact that there are three days named for astrological bodies: Monday (moon day), Sunday (sun day), and Saturday (Saturn day).

Thus, at one time, "disaster" meant bad ("dis") stars ("aster"). In other words, astrological charts indicated when you should probably call in sick to work. If something catastrophic occurred to you or to your community or to the entire world, many thought "disaster" (an unfavorable alignment of the stars) was to blame.

The scientific community lost its belief in astrology as a science in the late eighteenth century and replaced it with the empirical science of astronomy. As that happened, "disaster" stopped being related to the stars, but it kept its sense of "something awful happening."

D

discotheque

ORIGINAL MEANING: record collection
NEW DEFINITION: club that plays recorded music

The French word for library is "bibliotheque." As young people—
in France and elsewhere—became aficionados of recorded
music, they developed a word for their record collections: "disco"
(record) plus "theque" (collection).

By the mid-1950s, as rock 'n' roll began to hold sway, clubs
opened to which young people brought their records and
danced to them. By metonymy, the clubs themselves became
discotheques. (Metonymy occurs when you replace one object
with another closely related to it. For example, Brits talk about
"the crown" when they mean the monarchy. Yanks say "the White
House" when they mean the president.)

D

Anyway, thanks in part to Bardot and to French New Wave
cinema, France became the epicenter of world culture for a time.
Americans borrowed the word "discotheque," and opened their
own versions. By the mid-1960s, discotheques were a common
sight in American cities.

Then, thanks to America's proclivity to shorten words—and
probably due to many Americans' inability to spell "discotheque"
properly—the French word was shortened to "disco." The word
came to represent both the music *and* the clubs that played it,
and thus paved the way for Studio 54, the Village People, and,
ultimately, the backlash against disco that effectively killed it as a
music genre by the early 1980s.

───── *But Can You Dance to It?* ─────

Only two words in English—borrowed from French, of course—end in
the letters "theque." One is "discotheque," typically shortened to "disco."
Today—perhaps with a hint of irony, perhaps not—people still like to "go
retro" and dance to disco music.

The other "theque" word is known only to film snobs. A cinema-
theque is a place with a collection of art-house films that it screens regularly. Again, note that the word's ending suggests "collection." Beginning
in France in the 1930s, cinematheques have crossed the pond and can
be found in cities such as Los Angeles, San Francisco, Chicago, and
even a notable one in Charlottesville, Virginia, on the campus of the University of Virginia.

D

dogma

ORIGINAL DEFINITION: philosophical tenet (arguable)
NEW DEFINITION: belief many deem absolutely true and
inarguable

The ancient Greeks, known for their schools of philosophy, gave
English the word that became "dogma." Yet, most likely, Plato,
Aristotle, and others would be displeased with what has become of
the term.

Originally, dogmata (still an acceptable plural for dogma)
were ideas or philosophies people held and batted around at what
passed for cocktail parties in ancient Athens: "You believe a soul
exists? What an interesting dogma. My dogma is that there is no
such thing as a soul."

As Christianity gained an increasing presence in the world,
"dogma" was "borrowed" to describe the tenets held by the Christian faith. Oops. Now faith has entered the picture. Then, as

today, people clung to their beliefs and would not entertain the possibility that their beliefs might be misguided, incomplete, or just plain wrong.

Before long, dogmata were no longer ideas to discuss over a cup of wine. They were the source of war, religious schism, family destruction, and nation-building. By the way, "dogma" was considered a Greek word in English until the nineteenth century.

doll

ORIGINAL DEFINITION: diminutive of Dorothy
NEW DEFINITION: toy in the form of a human

D

The objects called dolls have been around for at least 4,000 years. Primitive ones have been found in Egyptian tombs. Articulated dolls wearing clothing have been dated to 200 years before Christ.

Nonetheless, the word "doll" is only a little over 300 years old, and it hasn't always meant a child's plaything. Initially, it was a nickname for Dorothy, in the way that Molly is a nickname for Mary.

Before it referred to something little girls played with, a "doll" was something big, grown-up men, um, played with. The word became interchangeable with "slattern" or "slut," most likely because "Doll" was such a common nickname at the time.

As other words were used to describe ladies of the evening, "doll" lost its connection to the, um, midnight arts. "Doll" became a word for a child's toy around 1700. Later in the eighteenth century, "doll" became a putdown for women. To call someone a doll was to suggest that she was as empty-headed as a child's plaything. The word still has a pejorative ring when used in place of a woman's name.

doom

ORIGINAL DEFINITION: a law; a judgment
NEW DEFINITION: destruction; ruin

Originally, "doom" was a secular word that referred to laws.

Christianity played the biggest role in dooming "doom," because of the Last Judgment. On this particular "doomsday," believers think that Jesus Christ will come down and pass judgment on everyone. For most people, that day probably won't be a very good one. Not a Christian? Oh, too bad. Zap! Stopped going to church? What a shame! Zap! Whether or not you believe in the Last Judgment, the connection between "doom" and destruction was formed and remains.

More modern laws have also been partners with destruction. *Plessy v. Ferguson*, anyone? This late nineteenth-century law made segregation acceptable, robbed African Americans of any rights they earned during Reconstruction, and immeasurably set back the course of human rights in the United States.

The intended—or unintended—consequences of some laws helped "doom" take on its present, best-known meaning as a partner for "gloom."

D

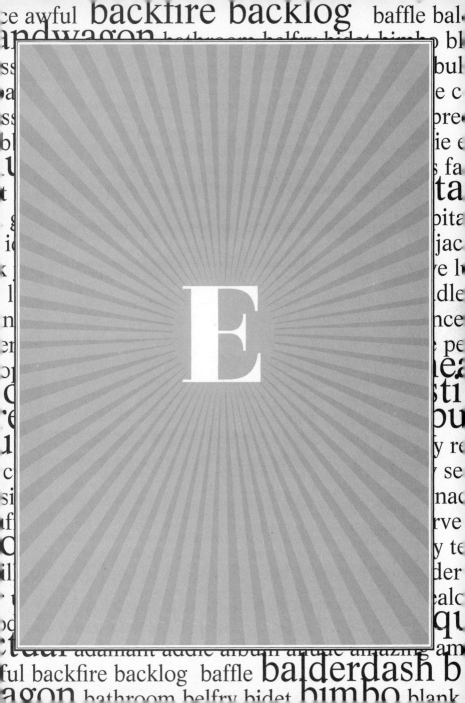

eager

ORIGINAL DEFINITION: sharp (as in sour); sharp (as in keen)
NEW DEFINITION: enthusiastic

"Eager" used to have many meanings, mainly based on the root words from which it derived. One root had mostly negative connotations: harsh, bitter, sour. Another root was positive: lively, active. A third root word sounds downright belligerent. It had meanings like sharp, piercing, and zealous. Thus, when the word first appeared in English, it had a mixture of meanings. It could signify anger, or it could signify any ardent feelings.

By the fourteenth century, English speakers decided to resolve all these different meanings into a new one that only tangentially seems related to its roots. The word "eager" became a synonym for "zealous." After all, someone eager is probably also ardent, and thus zealous. "Eager" carried this sharp-edged slant into the nineteenth century.

Nowadays, "eager" is a mostly positive word. When someone shows *too* much eagerness, there are new words—less positive—to describe him or her: overeager, sycophant, lackey, and brown-noser.

---

economy

ORIGINAL DEFINITION: household management
NEW DEFINITION: financial resources of a country

Once upon a time, "economy" dealt specifically with the management of an individual household. The Greek word that led to "economy" meant just that: household management.

Of course, even in its earliest days, finances played a part in taking care of one's family. But in a largely agricultural world, that was only one among many responsibilities. There was also the

need to care for animals, to assign various tasks, to gather up people to help with harvests, to educate one's children at home, etc.

The widespread exploration of the 1400s and 1500s led to
global interconnectedness. For example, gold discoveries in Latin
America in the 1500s began a shift toward the gold standard in
many countries.

That's how, by the middle of the 1600s, "economy" began to
have an explicitly financial meaning. If one spoke of household
economy, then it meant "household resources." In most cases,
however, the word now refers to the financial resources of a
country.

—— *More Economies* ——

Ultimately, "economy" overflowed its banks, so to speak, and led to the
creation of two terms. Microeconomics deals with financial resources
within households and individual businesses, while macroeconomics
deals with the entire world's financial resources.

E

edify

ORIGINAL DEFINITION: to build; construct
NEW DEFINITION: to instruct someone in matters of education or
morality

Maybe you've wondered about the connection between "edify"
and "edifice." Cleary, they're related words, but one has to with
buildings and one doesn't. It turns out that there *is* a connection
between "edifice" and "edify," but it's been lost to history.

In the fourteenth century, "edify" focused on buildings. Monks
might "edify" a church. A king might "edify" a castle. The word

suggested building something. Period. Of course, it didn't take too long for people to ascribe to the word a metaphorical sense of "build someone's faith." In medieval times, the Church reigned supreme. Education meant *religious* education. Thus, nothing was more important to the Church than creating structures of faith—both literally and in people's minds.

As time went on, "edify" came loose from its foundation. The word stopped referring primarily to structures and began to refer almost exclusively to people. Though the word still suggests instructing someone morally, it's most often heard today in a non-secular manner.

eerie

ORIGINAL DEFINITION: fearful; timid
NEW DEFINITION: frightening due to a strange or unexpected quality

E

For about 400 years, someone might describe you as "eerie" if you spooked easily. One of the word's roots means "unmanly." Thus, "eerie" men were cowards.

As time went on, the word made a shift from denoting someone who is afraid to describing something that *causes* fear. Basically, it just transformed from a passive to an active word. By the turn of the nineteenth century, "eerie" became the perfect word to describe everything from gothic horror novels to coyote howls to Theremin music.

If you ever find yourself in the Scottish Highlands, then you'll discover that "eerie" maintains its original meaning. To this day, "eerie" is a synonym of "afraid." So, don't start any fights in the local pub by using the word incorrectly.

egregious

ORIGINAL DEFINITION: exceptional or outstanding, in a good way
NEW DEFINITION: exceptional or outstanding, in a bad way

Originally, "egregious" simply meant exceptional or outstanding. It was an "attaboy" word. "Good fellow," one might have said circa 1550, "that was an egregious display of archery skill." And the recipient of the remark might have beamed with delight.

By the end of the same century, however, the same "compliment" might have led to fisticuffs, a donnybrook, a scuffle because by 1600, "egregious" had almost entirely adopted its new meaning of "outstandingly bad."

The reason for the change? Something with which teenagers the world over are very familiar: sarcasm.

Over time, many, many people of the sixteenth century began to use the word "egregious" the same way people today might say, "Great job," and really mean, "Rotten job." The negative sense of the word caught on, and "egregious" stopped being complimentary.

E

empty

ORIGINAL DEFINITION: unmarried
NEW DEFINITION: vacant; containing nothing

Here's proof that marriage is more fulfilling than the single life. At one time, "empty" meant, variously: idle, at leisure, and without obligation. But one of its principal definitions was "unmarried." Yep, the unmarried life once was, literally, the "empty life."

The word evolved over the centuries to focus on a lack in general, rather than on those lacking lasses or lads. The semantic shift isn't too difficult to follow. All of "empty's" original meanings suggest vacant hours or a life containing no one but you. Thus, "empty" came to mean vacant or void by the end of the Middle Ages.

—— *Not So Empty After All* ——

For such an "empty" word, "empty" has had a pretty full life. In the 1600s, the expression "empty-handed," meaning lacking money or goods, came along. And in the 1980s, the term "empty nester" became a vogue way to describe parents whose children have grown up and moved away.

enthusiasm

ORIGINAL DEFINITION: divine inspiration
NEW DEFINITION: excitement; eagerness

At one time, if a person was in the grip of "enthusiasm," it meant that he had been possessed by the divine inspiration of God himself. In fact, he would have been in the grip of religious ecstasy: speaking in tongues, writhing on the ground, etc.

Then along came the Puritans. They thought all that "religious ecstasy" was overdoing it. People, God forbid, might be . . . enjoying themselves in church! Wasn't there something a little, well, lewd about all that writhing around?! Thus, for a time, "enthusiasm" gained a pejorative ring, suggesting excessive expression of religious emotions and, by extension, *any* disproportionate display of emotion.

The general public rescued "enthusiasm" by the eighteenth century. It lost its connection to religious zeal, but it gained a non-pejorative sense of excitement, interest, or eagerness. Of course, "enthusiasm" can still be pejorative if, say, your fishing fanatic buddy drags you out of bed at 5:30 A.M. on a Saturday because "that's when the good ones are biting."

---

exorcise

ORIGINAL DEFINITION: to invoke spirits
NEW DEFINITION: to banish spirits

From 1400 to 1600, "exorcise" could mean either using demons for nefarious (or profit-making) purposes, *or* for casting demons out of poor, unsuspecting innocents. But an exorcism was often simply an opportunity for someone to invoke spirits in order to get them to do his or her bidding. By 1600, the word began to refer almost exclusively to getting rid of demons. It became synonymous with "casting out devils," one of Christ's New Testament miracles: "But if I by the Spirit of God cast out devils, then is the kingdom of God come upon you" (Matthew 12:29).

Exorcism has been a staple of horror films at least since Linda Blair used a crucifix for purposes God never intended in the 1973 film, *The Exorcist.* As a result, most people are familiar with an exorcism ceremony. To wit: A demon has inhabited a formerly nice person, making him or her evil, and a priest/shaman/holy person is called in to throw that infernal sucker right back into hell.

E

---

expletive

ORIGINAL MEANING: "empty" words used in writing
NEW MEANING: profanity; swearword

The original definition of "expletive" refers to words like "it" when "it" doesn't have a clear antecedent (a word to which "it" refers).

For example, consider the sentence "It is stupid of you to skip class." "It" is a pronoun, yet, in that sentence, "it" doesn't refer to anything. You should instead say, "To skip class is stupid." But nobody really talks—or writes—this way. If you do, you're an egghead. (No one likes you. Get over yourself.)

For people who study linguistics, an expletive is still a "filler" word, but for most, "expletive" is a word that means "dirty word" or "profanity." Some credit Sir Walter Scott with introducing "expletive" as an alternative to "offensive" words. But as far as mainstream usage, the English language has Richard Nixon to thank. The man who gave the world Watergate and a lasting distrust of politicians also bequeathed the modern sense of the word "expletive." Transcripts from the tapes Nixon secretly made while in the White House are filled with the expression "expletive deleted." Nixon being quite the pottymouth, the phrase was so omnipresent that it associated (perhaps forever) "expletive" with "four-letter word."

E

—— *Minced Oaths* ——

When you mince something for a recipe, you cut it into very small pieces. When you "mince an oath," you take a word or phrase that's exceptionable and make it acceptable for general audiences. Thus, "minced oath" is the term etymologists have given to expletives that have been rendered toothless.

- The "d word": darn, dang, doggone
- The "s word": shoot, sugar, shucks
- The "h word": heck, H-E-double hockey sticks
- The "g word": gosh, goodness, golly, goldang, goldarn
- The "f word": flipping, freaking, effing, fricking

explode

ORIGINAL DEFINITION: to drive someone off a stage with clapping and rude noises
NEW DEFINITION: to blast; detonate; blow up

Originally, "explode" comes from a Latin root that means literally "outclap." The idea goes something like this. You're watching a play, and you think the play sucks or the acting is terrible. So, you start to clap loudly, hiss, and stamp your feet, all in an effort to get those bozos off the stage.

Even after the word entered English, it still carried this ancient meaning. Critics would write about actors being "exploded" off the stage, and they didn't mean someone blew them into tiny bits (even if the critics thought this would have been a worthy response to a putrid performance). The connection between the stage and a grenade is the loud, fright-inducing noise.

The word didn't gain its primary present-day meaning, of a violent, destructive burst, until the end of the nineteenth century. Nowadays, no one would ever assume a connection between bad acting and dirty bombs, but, historically, there it is.

E

fabulous

ORIGINAL DEFINITION: mythical; legendary
NEW DEFINITION: wonderful; extraordinary

If you look at this word, you can see that "fable" seems to be part of it. Fables are fictional stories that include universal truths. In that way, they're akin to myths. Myths are stories once believed true, now believed fictional, that give the origin of worlds, cultures, etc.

Thus, "fabulous" was used to describe objects, animals, and people you would find in myths or fables. Dragons were "fabulous." The exploits of early European kings were "fabulous." Alchemy turned out to be "fabulous."

The transformation of this word is straightforward. Mythical and legendary kings, for example, were larger than life. They were like ancient superheroes. When stories were told about them, listeners were filled with wonder. They found these heroes' actions extraordinary—literally beyond the ordinary.

Thus, by the early modern era, "fabulous" focused on the feelings of wonder people experienced when hearing fables and myths, rather than on the myths and fables themselves.

F

facial

ORIGINAL DEFINITION: face-to-face
NEW DEFINITION: spa service

Long before it was something offered in beauty salons and spas, "facial" was a word that meant "face-to-face." For example, "I had a facial discussion with John about the price of hogs." Or, "Would you have a facial meeting with me regarding the potential for our courtship?"

Somewhere around the early part of the 1800s, folks started to use "facial" when they meant "of the face." For example, "I see you have a facial blemish."

About 100 years later, beauticians began to offer facials to well-heeled customers. Facial masks exfoliated, cleansed, and moisturized —all things "of the face."

Finally, sometime during the second half of the twentieth century, "facial" became a term used to describe certain acts in pornographic videos. This is the type of facial with which men are most likely to be familiar.

---

fact

ORIGINAL DEFINITION: feat; evil deed
NEW DEFINITION: information known or believed to be true

This word's Latin roots suggest "something done," an accomplishment. But in its earliest use, "fact" also had a negative connotation. That sense is still captured in legalese like "accessory after the fact."

Since a "fact" once meant an occurrence or action, especially an "evil" one, then people probably talked about what had happened. In those days before instant communication, wagging tongues were the principal source of information. Most likely, then as now, not everything presented as "fact" actually was verifiably true. But, then as now, *how* correct each account was probably didn't matter. Once the word had spread, the "fact" might as well have been true. So the definition morphed into a report of something that was indeed true. The fact that a "fact" wasn't necessarily always factual didn't preclude everyone from accepting it as gospel truth.

As was so aptly said in *The Man Who Shot Liberty Valance*, "When the legend becomes fact, print the legend."

---

fanatic

ORIGINAL DEFINITION: possessed by a deity
NEW DEFINITION: someone who is overzealous or overenthusiastic

The Latin word that gave the English language "fanatic" once simply meant "temple." Just like today, there were people in ancient Rome who went to church every time the doors were open. Thus, over time, the Latin word began to refer to pious people.

Sometimes, these really pious people were so inspired by their faith that they didn't wash regularly or they mumbled to themselves or they jerked about spasmodically. In short, they acted as if they were possessed. Thus, the last meaning of the Latin root was "one who acts possessed by a deity."

When the word entered English, during the sixteenth century, "fanatic" still specifically focused on religious people who were maybe possessed by a little *too* much religion. By the seventeenth century, "fanatic" broadened to include anyone who acted "possessed" by an interest in anything. While no longer believed possessed literally, these present-day "fanatics" love their sports team, television show, or favorite musician to a more-than-is-healthy extent.

F

farce

ORIGINAL DEFINITION: stuffing (food)
NEW DEFINITION: program or play featuring broad comedy

What does the stuff you put in a turkey at Thanksgiving have to do with outrageous comedy? The answer can be found, of all places, inside the doors of the medieval Roman Catholic Church.

Until the 1400s, "farce" was a culinary term that meant stuffing. Thus, people enjoyed "farce-filled" guinea fowl (or whatever bird folks ate in medieval England).

At roughly the same time, many priests took liberties with the liturgical text. The liturgy during a Catholic Mass then, as now, was formulaic, but (also then, as now) at various portions during the Mass, a priest could interject his own message or information. He would offer it in the vernacular rather than in Latin. Thus, people began to call this nonliturgical, non-Latinate material "farce" because it was like the "stuffing" in the Mass.

This sense of "farce" was borrowed when churches put on mystery plays. This early form of theater depicted miracles (mysteries) from the Bible. Often, actors would engage in comic relief in the middle of these plays. Again, this buffoonery (see entry for "buffoon") was like the "stuffing" within the mystery play. Eventually, these comic interludes became so popular that they "spun off" into a genre of their own, which still exists today to the delight of immature men everywhere.

F

—— *Farce and Slapstick* ——

Americans tend to associate the word "farce" with the word "slapstick." Slapstick's golden age (which sounds like an oxymoronic concept) included Charlie Chaplin, the Marx Brothers, W. C. Fields, and (of course) The Three Stooges. Nowadays, the comedies of Judd Apatow and Tyler Perry keep the slapstick tradition alive. But where does the word "slapstick" come from?

Italian theater produced "commedia dell'arte" in the sixteenth century. This early form of comedy used clowns (see entry for "clown") to ape the mannerisms of typical stereotypes of the day: stuffed shirts, cowardly military leaders, etc.

One prop used during these early farces was the "bataccio," translated into English as "slapstick." The "bataccio" made a lot of noise when one hit someone with it, though it actually caused no harm. Nonetheless, the reaction of a character hit with a "bataccio" and the loud sound it made combined to make audiences roar with laughter. Thus, "slapstick" became broad physical humor.

filibuster

F

ORIGINAL DEFINITION: pirate
NEW DEFINITION: delaying tactic often used in the Senate

You've probably heard the word "freebooter," which is a synonym for "pirate." A pirate gets free booty (the type that means loot, not the type associated with physical companionship) because he steals it. Another common term of old was "filibuster." Both "freebooter" and "filibuster" came from the same Danish word, "vrijbuiter." "Freebooter" became one English variation. Another, via French and Spanish, entered English as "filibuster." So, at first, a "filibuster" was a pirate.

The word first gained an American connection in the mid-nineteenth century. "Filibuster" was the name given to U.S. citizens who organized ersatz militias and attempted to gain possession of Latin American countries.

Thus, "filibuster" began to mean anyone who used belligerent means for his or her own gain. At the same time the word was used to describe would-be despots, some wags began to use the term to describe the time-honored delaying tactic used on the floor of the Senate. After all, senators who used speeches as delaying tactics to try and influence votes were "pirating" the legislative decision.

flippant

ORIGINAL DEFINITION: talkative
NEW DEFINITION: displaying inappropriate levity; an inability to recognize the gravity of a situation

At the turn of the seventeenth century, someone "flippant" was someone who wouldn't shut up. The word lost its original meaning for metaphorical reasons. Someone who likes to hear the sound of his own voice isn't really paying serious attention to yours. Thus, "flippant" started to describe the actions of someone making a wiseass joke whenever you start getting serious. Nowadays, a flippant person is one who makes jokes when, say, you're trying to get advice about how to solve a difficult problem: "Hey, Bob, my wife and I argue all the time." Bob replies, "Just kill her."

F

flirt

ORIGINAL DEFINITION: to treat with contempt; sneer or jeer at;
one who does these things

NEW DEFINITION: to engage in playful courtship; one who
engages in playful courtship

In Shakespeare's day, "flirt" was associated with saucy, impertinent
women. Singles bars didn't exist 500 years ago, but if they had,
a young man being "flirted with" by a comely wench would have
known he'd go home alone. Why? To be "flirted" with was to be
insulted by a woman we likely would call independent and discern-
ing today.

Over time, however, "flirting" became something positive.
This is due to the fact that flirting often takes the form of playful
insults. After all, a cliché that has created a zillion romantic comedies dictates that men and women who treat one another with
contempt are in fact completely in gooey, syrupy love with one
another.

garbage

ORIGINAL DEFINITION: parts of an animal not eaten
NEW DEFINITION: disposable material

Now that we have entire ersatz nations made out of garbage, swirling about in the world's oceans and killing aquatic life, it's easy to forget that the world was not always infiltrated by tossed disposable goods.

Consider medieval times. People didn't have paper towels, disposable diapers, entertainment magazines, or those damnable plastic shopping bags that everyone knows we should eschew in favor of reusable bags. It's just that, dammit, it's so easy to forget to bring them in to the grocery store!

Anyway, for the early part of its life in English, "garbage" referred mostly to parts of an animal that couldn't be used for another purpose. There wasn't a whole lot of other "trash." But all those animal parts? You couldn't eat them, wear them, or use them to construct things. In short, they were useless and disposable.

The connection, therefore, already existed between "garbage" and "worthless stuff." That meaning was bolstered when people got "garbage" and "garble" mixed-up (see entry for "garble"). "Garble" meant to sift through spices in order to filter out impurities. By the 1600s, "garbage" referred to any pile of useless stuff that, even then, began to clog up the planet.

G

garble

ORIGINAL DEFINITION: to sift
NEW DEFINITION: to confuse stories or words so much that meaning is confused or lost

At one time, the word "garble" referred specifically to spices. A spice trader would stop at a Mediterranean port and purchase a barrel of some spice. In order to make sure he wasn't being cheated, the spice trader would sift through the spice merchant's wares and make sure they weren't filled with impurities or fillers.

If the merchant was dishonest, sifting spices would create piles of various unrelated parts. Sifting *language* can have the same metaphoric result.

Think of the game "telephone." One person whispers something into someone's ear, who whispers it into the ear of her neighbor, who whispers it to the next person. Eventually, the information makes its way around the room, but often in a dramatically altered state.

Why does the meaning get lost? Well, people can only remember so much information at a time. They choose the bits they think are most important before they send the message on. Thus, by "sifting" through the information, they "garble" it.

— Garbled Lyrics —

People have garbled the lyrics of even the most popular songs, and sometimes the results are pretty funny. Here are just a few examples.

- John Fogerty's southern accent via Southern California has led some people to mishear a particular line from "Bad Moon Rising." Instead of "There's a bad moon on the rise," some believe he's singing, "There's a bathroom on the right."
- Michael Jackson's emotive voice has led people to garble a line from "Billie Jean." Jackson repeatedly wails that "the kid is not my son," but some swear he's saying, "The chair is not my son."
- Christmas carols aren't immune to garbled lyrics. Consider this line from "We Wish You a Merry Christmas": "Now bring us some figgy pudding." Since figs are no longer a big Yuletide favorite, some believe the line is, "Now bring us some frigging pudding."

G

gentle

ORIGINAL DEFINITION: well-born
NEW DEFINITION: mild-mannered; polite

Once upon a time, if you were "gentle," you were rich. You were from a "good" family. The root of the word suggests "beget," as in, springing forth from an established or "good" lineage.

If they were well-born, the rich were the "one-percenters" of their day, and thus, they were pretty much focused on themselves, what was good for themselves, and what was most expedient for themselves. Damn the peasants. Let them eat cake.

Nonetheless, to this day, many ascribe to the "well-born" a preoccupation with etiquette, which is really just egotistically excessive good manners used like a performance.

Over time, as lineages began to split, and peasants started to revolt, the word "gentle" became more egalitarian. It began to refer to people—well-born or not—who exhibited characteristics associated (rightly or wrongly) with the rich: good manners, refinement, politeness, amiability, etc. Nowadays, the main connection "gentle" has to its hoity-toity roots is the word "gentleman."

gestation

ORIGINAL DEFINITION: riding on horseback
NEW DEFINITION: the period of time, from conception until birth, during which a female person or animal carries her child; pregnancy

What's with words related to horses? A bidet used to be a small horse, and the action of riding it gave rise to the current meaning of the word (see entry for "bidet"). And gestation? During the sixteenth century, it meant the act of riding on horseback for exercise. Now it has nothing at all to do with horses . . . except for mares carrying foals.

How did the modern meaning of "gestation" undergo such an unusual birth? The answer is in the root of the word. It comes from a Latin word meaning "to carry" or "to bear." In addition, when you ride a horse, the horse is "bearing" you. Thus, the "seed" of the modern sense of the word exists in both its origin and its Middle–Ages meanings. By the seventeenth century, "gestation" referred only to maturation and to ideas. Horses had ridden off into the sunset.

girl

ORIGINAL DEFINITION: a young child of either gender
NEW DEFINITION: a young female child

When "girl" first began to appear in writing, during the mid-thirteenth century, it could refer to a youth of either gender. By the mid-sixteenth century, the word chose a gender and came to refer specifically to young females.

The reason for the shift is not entirely clear. The word "boy" meant specifically a male child as early as 1400, and that may be why the change was made. If there was one word that meant "young male," then it stood to reason it would be convenient to have another word that meant "young female." Since "girl" could mean either gender, it was likely just expedient to choose one in order to have a contrast for "boy."

The word's origin offers another possibility for why "girl" came to refer to females. One of "girl's" origin words means "dress" or "article of clothing." Since young ladies then, as now, tend to pay

G

more attention to their clothing than young men do, the word gained a feminine connection.

---

gossip

ORIGINAL DEFINITION: godparent
NEW DEFINITION: One who discusses other people's business

Originally, "gossips" referred to one's closest acquaintances or even family members. The Old English word that led to "gossip" meant "god-related." In other words, if you choose, say, Bob down the street to be your child's "gossip," or godparent, then you became related to Bob through God.

By the Middle Ages, "gossips" weren't just godparents. They were any close relatives or friends. Often, the word was used to describe women who came together for births. As they waited for the blessed moment to arrive, they engaged in idle chatter. Ultimately, "gossip" became associated with this idle chatter more than with being a godparent.

By Shakespeare's time, a gossip was what he or she is today: a busybody putting his or her nose where it doesn't belong.

---

gout

G

ORIGINAL DEFINITION: to drop
NEW DEFINITION: painful inflammation of the joints, especially the joint of the big toe

The word "gout" comes from French via Latin and meant "drop" originally. The connection between the old and new meanings is rooted in outdated concepts of medicine; although, in truth, physicians of old weren't too far off in their diagnoses. Gout is a disease that causes excruciating swelling in the joints, though 50 percent of its sufferers feel the red-hot, searing pain in the joint of their big toes. Doctors of old believed that gout was caused when waste products "dropped" from blood and settled in the joints. Doctors knew about gravity, so it made sense to them that most sufferers felt pain in one of the body's lowest joints.

These doctors didn't know why some people's blood "dropped" and others didn't. They did note, however, that many gout patients were wealthy and imbibed alcohol regularly. That's why some called gout "the rich man's disease."

Medical science today knows that the culprit that leads to gout is an excess of uric acid. Too much alcohol—or fructose or meat—creates an excess of uric acid in the blood that the bloodstream deposits in various joints of the body. Until recently, only the rich would have been able to have a diet high in meat and spirits.

—— *Gout Stool* ——

Gout became rampant in the eighteenth century as the leisure class gained in size. Men of means spent their time eating rich foods and drinking too much stout, and as a result they contracted gout. In those days, no one was quite sure how the disease occurred. Yet folks with the disease realized they could alleviate suffering by elevating the gout-ridden foot.

Well, these pampered pashas couldn't just put their feet up on a chair or a stack of books. Oh no. How bourgeois! Thus, furniture makers of the time created gout stools, which were simply fabric-covered stools that allowed one to prop up one's feet in style. Occasionally, these antiques pop up on eBay. They sell for anywhere from $25 to over $100.

G

grin

ORIGINAL DEFINITION: showing the teeth due to pain or anger
NEW DEFINITION: show the teeth in a smile

Sometimes it can be painful to hold a grin for too long, which is why most people's family photos are so unintentionally creepy. Those aren't grins; they're faces of discomfort. The pain that leads to cheesy yearbook and photo album smiles is appropriate to the word's original meaning.

The words that originated "grin" mean such things as whine, howl, or cry. In other words, "grins" were more like what we now call grimaces. Your teeth are bared, yes, but not in joy or contentment or even to satisfy a photographer's demand. Instead, your teeth are pulled back in pain or possibly in anger.

By the late fourteenth century, "grin" began to change in meaning. The modern sense of the word most likely came via the sense of a forced smile, which often masks pain or anger. By the early modern era, grins were awaiting the day they could become caught awkwardly in photo albums, yearbooks, and newspapers.

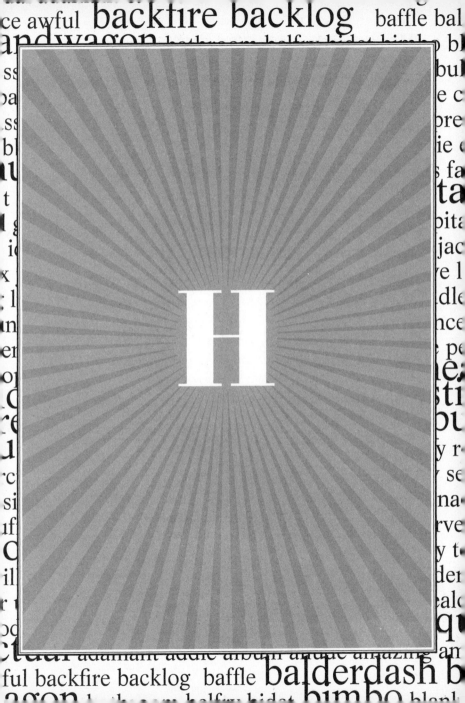

harlot

ORIGINAL DEFINITION: tramp; vagabond (male)
NEW DEFINITION: prostitute (female)

In Chaucer's day, there wasn't necessarily anything wrong with being called a "harlot." The word often was used for traveling street performers and poets, the men (NOTE: men) who provided entertainment in a world sadly devoid of reruns, moronic tweets, and viral videos of kittens doing cute things.

Even then, during the middle of the Middle Ages, the word could have a pejorative ring. If a man was merely a "tramp," someone who walked from town to town begging, rather than performing, for his supper, then he, too, would be called a "harlot."

By the dawn of the 1400s, the word began to shift genders, and it was as an alternative to "whore." Some women, um, plied their trade among different communities, or (male) harlots got, um, lonely on the road and sought female companionship for a price. Thus, a connection was made between the "old" harlots and the "new" harlots.

The main culprit for transforming "harlots" from male street performers to female sheet performers was early Modern English translations of the Bible. "Harlot" often was used as a euphemism for the harsher-sounding (for the time) words like "whore" or "strumpet."

haywire

ORIGINAL DEFINITION: wire used to bind hay
NEW DEFINITION: crazy; erratic

As America tamed the West during the last years of the nineteenth century, people started making a lot of hay while the sun shone (literally). They used the hay to feed animals, to stuff cushions, to insulate, and for any number of other things.

One convenient way to keep hay stored was to form it into bales and then hold it together with wire made for that purpose. From the beginning, people began to use "haywire" for all sorts of purposes its manufacturers never intended.

People used haywire to repair nearly everything, and they used it to hold together more than just hay. Herein lies the seed for "haywire's" transformation from "hay-binding wire" to something that is crazy or erratic.

Haywire wasn't meant for heavy-duty repairs, so "projects" that used it often fell apart without warning. Haywire was never meant to, say, bind logs, so huge piles of logs might break their jury-rigged bonds and "go haywire." Nowadays, the word is rarely, if ever, used to describe material that binds hay.

---

heartburn

ORIGINAL DEFINITION: lust
NEW DEFINITION: chest pain caused by acid reflux

Some guys still give ladies heartburn, figuratively speaking. Eight hundred years ago, however, men would have loved to give damsels "heartburn." After all, it meant "lust."

During the Middle Ages, the heart already was associated with love. Hundreds of years before Christ, Aristotle suggested that the heart was the center of emotions. Thus, something that made your heart "burn" filled you with lust. But your heart doesn't just burn for amatory reasons.

By the fourteenth century, "heartburn" suggested another emotion, namely, anger or hatred.

H

However, by the fifteenth century, "heartburn" began being used to describe that particular burning sensation that can follow the consumption of a spicy meal. Since the word "heartburn" already existed, it was a simple move to use it to describe a physical sensation that literally made you feel like your heart was on fire. Writers may still talk about how someone's actions caused another's heart to "burn with rage" and that sort of thing, but they aren't likely to use the word "heartburn" to describe this feeling.

---

heckle

ORIGINAL DEFINITION: to comb with a heckle
NEW DEFINITION: to tease or make fun of, especially a public figure or performer

A "heckle" was a type of brush used to clean certain crops, such as hemp or flax. Once the crop had been "heckled"—i.e., had a heckle used on it—it could be taken to market and sold or could be made into other products.

By the late 1700s, people began to use the verb "heckle" metaphorically. When one "heckled"—in the old-fashioned sense—he or she ruffled the flax or hemp in order to remove impurities. Thus, when people "ruffled" politicians or public speakers by asking harsh or insistent questions, people began to say these public figures were being "heckled."

By the late nineteenth century, most "hecklers" didn't ask tough, pointed questions. They attempted to make fools of public figures by teasing them and trying to throw them off message through rude attempts at humor.

H

As standup comedy became an industry in the mid-twentieth century, "heckle" began to forge a connection with people who try to "outdo" those onstage, and it lost its connection to anything useful.

hospital

ORIGINAL DEFINITION: poorhouse; inn
NEW DEFINITION: place in which one receives medical treatment

"Hospital" conjures up scary images of doctors, gurneys, x-rays, and very long needles. But at one time, a "hospital" was not a medical center at all. It was a place in which the poor and needy lived.

You don't need to be an etymologist to see the "visual" connection among words like hospital, hotel, hostel, and hospice. All these words share Latin roots that refer to foreigners or strangers. They are places for temporary shelter.

Over time, a hospital stopped being a place for the poor and became an inn, a place where a visitor was shown hospitality. Over time, the word "hospital" became specialized, just like its "cousins," hotel and hostel. A hotel is a place to stay for a while when you travel. A hospital is a place to stay for awhile because you're sick.

hussy

ORIGINAL DEFINITION: contraction of housewife
NEW DEFINITION: impertinent woman of loose morals

"Hussy" was once an early English contraction of the Middle English "husewif," or "housewife." "Hussies" were women who stayed home, raised the kids, milked the cows, and did as they were told. Around the turn of the seventeenth century, "hussy" began to be used to describe any woman or girl. She didn't have to be a housewife or even married.

As the word broadened in meaning, it started to be used in a pejorative sense. Class distinctions were at the root of the semantic shift. Women of the lower classes such as milkmaids, farm workers, and spinsters (see entry for "spinster") were typically called "hussies." Then, as now, many believed that the poor were poor because they deserved to be. They must be lazy and shiftless, or they wouldn't be poor. In short, they're bad.

Thus, by the end of the eighteenth century, "hussy" was a completely negative word. A (shameless) hussy was (and is) impertinent, disagreeable, and possesses loose morals.

hysterical

ORIGINAL DEFINITION: of the womb
NEW DEFINITION: really funny; overwrought

The word "hysterical" derives from the Greek word for womb, and initially, it referred to the womb itself. Then, (male) scientists of old believed they had discovered a neurotic condition peculiar to women, when they acted odd or "crazy." "Hmm, how come women are like this and men aren't?" they pondered. (Of course, no one seemed to think men had a problem even though they waged war regularly.)

Anyway, these ancients might finally have said, "Eureka!" (The word "eureka" was coined by the Greeks), the problem must be in the uterus! Men don't have them; women do. That's it! Pregnancy was sometimes "prescribed" to make women less "hysterical."

H

By the early twentieth century, "hysterical" came to mean funny or emotionally overpowering because of its association with uncontrollable emotions.

Of course, the related word, "hysteria," still suggests a neurotic condition, but it's no longer limited to just one gender.

H

iconoclast

ORIGINAL DEFINITION: destroyer of images
NEW DEFINITION: one who eschews established beliefs

Tension between the Roman Catholic and Eastern Orthodox branches of early Christianity gave English the modern word "bugger" (see entry for "bugger"). It also bequeathed "iconoclast."

These two faiths split early, but most people don't know that they ever had any connection to one another. Greek Orthodox (Eastern Orthodoxy in America) priests can marry, for example. The Greek Orthodox Church doesn't believe in the Immaculate Conception of Mary (that she was conceived without sin). And they don't believe in having lots of religious imagery.

To this day, some insult Roman Catholics because they "worship statues." They actually don't worship statues, but their churches do contain a lot of icons, or religious images. That's been true for centuries.

During the eighth and ninth centuries, some members of the Eastern Orthodox Church began to go through Roman Catholic churches and destroy some of these icons. "Iconoclast" is an Anglicized version of Greek words that mean "icon breaker."

By the nineteenth century, some writers began to broaden the scope of "iconoclast." They used the term to describe anyone who rejected orthodox beliefs—orthodox with a small "o," that is, meaning beliefs that are common. Thus, if everyone says that the sky is blue and you say the sky is green, then you're an iconoclast. Or, some might say, merely a butthead.

idiot

ORIGINAL DEFINITION: layman; uneducated person
NEW DEFINITION: generic insult used to suggest someone lacks intelligence

Initially, the word "idiot" just referred to a layman, as opposed to a skilled worker, or it referred to an uneducated person, as opposed to someone who had attended a university. In other words, it was an elitist term, thrown at people considered rabble by the medieval version of the bourgeoisie.

By the early modern era, an "idiot" referred to a stupid person. Consider, for example, Shakespeare's famous line from *Macbeth,* "Life . . . is a tale, told by an idiot, full of sound and fury, signifying nothing." William Faulkner borrowed the line some 300 years later to title his book, and the Bard's words suggest that the terrible misfortunes one experiences in life occur because humanity is in the middle of an idiot's story.

In Faulkner's book, *The Sound and the Fury* (published in 1929), the first section is narrated by Benjy Compson, a thirty-three-year-old man with the intelligence level of a three-year-old. He is referred to as an "idiot," which, at that time, was a recently coined technical term for someone with very low intelligence. So, for that matter were "moron" and "imbecile" (see entries for "imbecile" and "moron"). Though in the early twentieth century, psychologists used "idiot" as a technical term, the word soon became a generic insult to someone's intelligence and stopped being used as an official medical designation.

I

—— *Athenian Idiots* ——

All people are born idiots. If you've ever found yourself believing this, then you are not a misanthrope. You're just a fan of ancient Greek philosophy.

The Athenians believed that all people are born idiots. To them, this meant that everyone is born selfish and focused on his or her own private affairs. The "cure" for idiocy was education. Once someone was educated, he or she attained citizenship. For Athenians, citizenship was a primary virtue. It meant one was focused on the good of all and not just on what was good for oneself.

ignoramus

ORIGINAL DEFINITION: legal term meaning "we do not know"
NEW DEFINITION: stupid person

"Ignoramus" is Latin for "we do not know," and it was a legal term until 1615. If a grand jury found that an indictment contained insufficient evidence, it would write "ignoramus" on the document. The meaning, basically, was "we don't recognize the validity of this indictment." It had nothing to do with stupidity . . . yet.

That changed in 1615, when Cambridge University produced a comedy by George Ruggle called *Ignoramus.* The title's eponymous character is a magistrate who thinks he's pretty smart. He isn't. As a result of his obvious (to the audience, not to him) willful ignorance, Mr. Ignoramus is subjected to all sorts of humiliating experiences.

The play was a rousing success. Almost immediately, therefore, "ignoramus" stopped being a legal term and became a word that denotes a foolish person, especially one who thinks he *isn't* foolish.

ill

ORIGINAL DEFINITION: evil
NEW DEFINITION: sick

"Ill's" origin is an Old Norse word meaning "malevolent" or "hurtful." In other words, one had to *choose* to be "ill." By the fifteenth century, the word began to develop the meaning with which it is typically associated today.

The change was metaphorical. If someone is "ill," meaning "evil," then they seem sick or unwell to those who are nice and agreeable. And often, evil actions create an unwell or ailing society.

The word "ill" underwent another shift in the 1980s, taking on its opposite meaning. Hip-hop artists, who became masters at taking negative words and making them positive ("dope," "sick") would say it was "ill." Sometimes, you'll still hear the word used that way.

—— *Scottish Ills* ——

While you might hear of someone absconding with ill-gotten gains, the word is rarely used today to describe someone who is bad . . . unless he lives in Scotland. The Scots still use "ill" as a synonym for evil. For the rest of the English-speaking world, however, "ill" means "an excuse not to go to work."

imbecile

ORIGINAL DEFINITION: weak; feeble
NEW DEFINITION: generic insult impugning someone's intelligence

"Imbecile" has gone through a couple of permutations. Its Latin word of origin meant literally "without a staff." Well, if you didn't

I

have a staff—the club variety, not the "walking stick" variety—then you were weaker than your opponent. Thus, the word meant "feeble" or "weak."

Jump ahead a couple thousand years, and psychologist Henry H. Goddard popularized the word "imbecile" as a technical term for people with an IQ of 26–50. Goddard also promoted the terms "idiot" and "moron" (see entries for "idiot" and "moron"). An "imbecile" was classified between a "moron" and an "idiot" on the intelligence scale.

Not long after "imbecile" gained some technical sheen, it was used as a generic, playground insult. Someone doing something others perceived as dumb—putting one's tongue on a metal pole in the dead of winter, for example—might be called an imbecile by his buddies.

As a result of its adoption as an insult, "imbecile" began to fall out of use in psychological circles, and, as a medical term, it has gone to non-politically-correct heaven.

inmate

ORIGINAL DEFINITION: temporary (voluntary) dweller
NEW DEFINITION: temporary or long-term (involuntary) dweller; prisoner

Being an "inmate" wasn't so bad, once upon a time. Originally, it just meant someone who resided temporarily in a hospital, hotel, or dorm room. Of course, if you were forced to eat campus chow during that stint in a dorm, you might have *felt* like you were in jail.

Some etymologists believe the word was formed by combining "inn" (hotel) and "mate" (companion). Others believe it's a combination of "mate" and "in" (inside). One way or the other, "inmate" was once a friendly word.

The word began to change in meaning in the nineteenth century, the same time as the modern prison system became popularized. Just remember, at one time, a prison was meant for a temporary stay, during which prisoners were to be rehabilitated and returned to society. Thus, "inmate" became a convenient, extant word one could use to describe these short-timers.

As the prison population began to grow and be filled more and more frequently with "permanent" residents, the word "inmate" lost its connection to voluntary activity and gained its association with involuntary confinement.

—— *Panopticon* ——

One father of the modern prison system is Jeremy Bentham (1748–1832). A proponent of utilitarianism, Bentham believed that anything that brings the most happiness to the most people is good. During his life, corporal punishment was common for many offenses, but Bentham believed that imprisonment was a better alternative. People would feel less pain, and they could be rehabilitated.

He devised a type of prison called a panopticon (meaning "see all"). Basically, it had a guard tower surrounded by several floors of prison cells. A guard could see every prisoner, but the inmates couldn't see where the guard was looking.

Panopticons never caught on, but one prison modeled on it was Cuba's Presidio Modelo. Opened in the 1920s, the prison closed in 1967. At one time, its most famous residents included young political dissidents Fidel and Raúl Castro.

inoculate

ORIGINAL DEFINITION: to graft; implant (gardening term)
NEW DEFINITION: to vaccinate

"Inoculate" had nothing to do with medicine until at least the early 1800s. Prior to that, it was a gardening or botanical term. The word's origin literally means "graft eye." The idea is that by grafting the "eye," or bud, of a plant into another, you can create a new strain of that plant. Even before Mendel "discovered" genetics in the nineteenth century, botanists knew you could get hardier strains of a plant by grafting different varieties together.

When a doctor inoculates you, she puts a tiny bit of a disease within you. The process is similar to grafting part of a plant onto another. As a result of this "grafting," your body is able to build up resistance to that disease so that if a full-blown case of it comes your way, you will likely be able to fight it off. Thus, until inoculations gained a medical association, "inoculate" meant simply to graft or implant and did not make children (and some wussy adults) cry.

intoxicate

ORIGINAL MEANING: to poison
NEW MEANING: to make drunk

When a bartender says, "Name your poison," she is being historically accurate.

The roots of this word go back to the Greek word "toxon," which meant "bow," as in "bow and arrow." The ancient Greeks often tipped their arrows with poison, called "toxikon." Latin borrowed these words and created the verb "intoxico," which meant to poison. By the time the word entered English, it had become "intoxicate."

Until the mid-fifteenth century, "intoxicate" had nothing to do with alcohol. One hundred years later, it had nothing to do with poison . . . except for alcohol poisoning, which remains a scourge of college campuses everywhere.

The shift occurred because many of the liquors common today began to be distilled in the second half of the fifteenth century (gin, schnapps, vodka, etc.). Until then, most people who drank imbibed wine. These new spirits had higher alcohol content than wine so people who drank them appeared poisoned.

When folks realized these drinkers weren't poisoned, just drunk, the verb "intoxicate"—and its adjective "intoxicated"—gained an explicit connection to drinking alcohol.

invest

ORIGINAL DEFINITION: to clothe; to dress
NEW DEFINITION: to commit money in hopes of a financial return

Originally, "invest" came from a Latin word meaning to clothe, cover, or surround. In the later Middle Ages, the word was used primarily to describe the literal or metaphorical act of putting on the vestments of an office. Someone says certain things, puts a funny hat on you, and voilà, you're the Pope.

By the early modern era, the word began to gain its modern sense. Most attribute the first use of "investing," as in gambling on an enterprise, to documents related to the East India Company, forerunner of the modern conglomerate. They traded everything from cotton and silk to opium.

Exactly how "putting on clothes" became "investing money" is not agreed upon by all etymologists. The principal contention is that the Latin word "investire" got mixed up with an Italian word of the same spelling. The Italian word has to do with clothing, but it does contain the modern meaning of "invest." The shift in meaning also is metaphorical. If you invest your money, you're "clothing" it in a business venture.

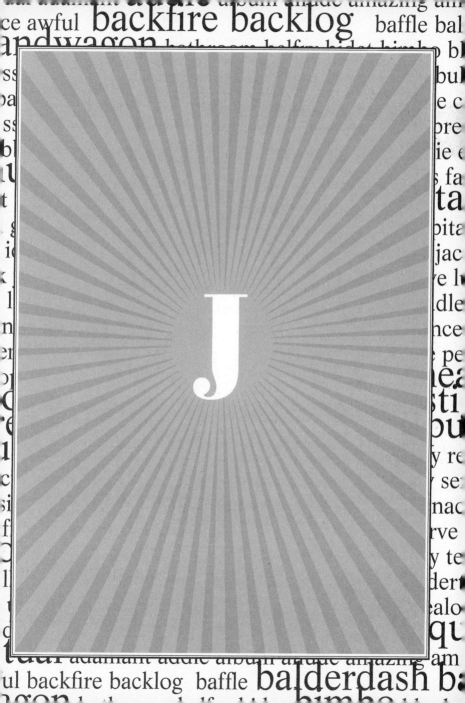

jack-in-the-box

ORIGINAL DEFINITION: thief; cheat
NEW DEFINITION: child's toy

J

At the time Shakespeare first picked up a quill, a "jack-in-the-box" was a thief who substituted empty boxes for boxes filled with goods. "Jack" already was a generic name for a man of low birth, a "nobody." That's the likely reason there was "jack" in the box. Anyone opening the box and finding nothing of value in it would have been in for a nasty surprise.

The toy, called a jack-in-the-box since at least the eighteenth century, acts on the same principle. An unsuspecting person—in this case, a child—figures out how to open the box and either screams in terror or squeals with delight.

One myth about how this particular toy developed traces the jack-in-the-box (even though it probably wasn't called that at the time) to the story of a thirteenth-century clergyman who threw the devil into a boot in order to protect a British village. Obviously, anyone who got too close to that boot was in for a nasty surprise.

—— *What on Earth Is a "Weasel,"* —— *and Why Does It Pop?*

The song linked inextricably to a jack-in-the-box is "Pop! Goes the Weasel." The original lyrics are as follows: "Half a pound of tupenny rice / Half a pound of treacle. / That's the way the money goes / Pop! Goes the weasel." Huh?!

Clearly, the song is not about the animal. If it "popped," then, presumably, that means it exploded. Gross. ➤

The song actually is about living in poverty, and its bizarre (to Yanks anyway) wording is related to Cockney slang. For Cockneys, "pop" is slang for pawn, and "weasel" is slang for a coat. Thus, after spending all your scant funds on food (rice, treacle), you've got to pawn your best Sunday coat.

J

jockey

ORIGINAL DEFINITION: boy; fellow
NEW DEFINITION: person who "pilots" a racehorse

In America, someone named Jonathan is sometimes nicknamed Jack, which others might amend to "Jackie" if they're close friends, for example. In Scotland and Northern England, "Jock" was common as a diminutive of Jonathan.

"Jock" or "jockey" became generically used to denote "some guy" or "that guy." By the sixteenth and seventeenth centuries, jockey (sometimes capitalized, sometimes not) began to get an unsavory reputation. If you called "some guy" a "jockey," you were saying he was possibly a card cheater, a tramp, or a crooked horse dealer, which is likely where "jockey" and "horse" first became acquainted.

By 1670, "jockey" was common parlance for a person who rides horses during races. Remember that one meaning of "jockey" was boy. Since jockeys typically are small in stature, the word may have easily attached itself to these vertically challenged horse racers.

juggernaut

ORIGINAL DEFINITION: wagon for Hindu god
NEW DEFINITION: unstoppable force or object

One of the principal Hindu gods is Vishnu. Sometimes he is worshipped directly, and at other times, he is worshipped through one of his ten avatars (physical incarnations), the most well-known (to Westerners) being Krishna.

Since at least the twelfth century, the community of Puri has celebrated Vishnu with an unusual annual ceremony. An image of the god is placed in a large, ceremonial wagon and pulled to another location across deep sand. The image of the god is called "Jagannatha," which English speakers later transformed into juggernaut.

Obviously, it's not easy to pull a heavy cart through deep sand. Vishnu's followers showed their devotion through just such a herculean task. When Westerners first encountered this tradition, they saw that Vishnu's followers often moved large objects out of the way rather than try to re-route the juggernaut. Sometimes, Westerners even observed people being crushed under the juggernaut's heavy wheels.

Stories filtered back home. These stories suggested that legions of Vishnu's followers sacrificed themselves (or were sacrificed) to Vishnu under the wheels of the juggernaut. Other tales were told of entire houses being dismantled to make way for the juggernaut.

Thus, a juggernaut became any large, implacable, unstoppable object. The ceremony that gave English the word "juggernaut" continues to this day.

juggler

ORIGINAL DEFINITION: wizard; sorcerer
NEW DEFINITION: one who keeps several objects in the air simultaneously

Now that juggling is one of those diversions—like card tricks—that bore jaded modern audiences, you may be interested to know that, at one time, a juggler was so much more than a person who keeps a few balls in the air. He was a wizard, a sorcerer, a practitioner of magic.

The word goes back to the dawn of the Middle Ages, and at that time, jugglers did pretty much what they do now. In addition to keeping several objects aloft, they might tell jokes or funny stories. After all, the Latin word at "juggler's" root means joker.

Jugglers got a bad name—as practitioners of magic—as the Middle Ages progressed. Religious fuddy-duddies went about accusing jugglers of being wizards and sorcerers and basically—to use a modern expression—harshed their mellow. The "art" stopped being performed publicly.

It never died, however. By the eighteenth century, the first modern circuses developed, and they were filled with jugglers. You'll still find jugglers in circuses today, but they're more likely to be tossing around chainsaws and machetes.

jury

ORIGINAL DEFINITION: temporary
NEW DEFINITION: group that decides a legal verdict

"Juries" used to come in two types: noun and adjective. The noun always has had legal overtones, while the adjective suggested makeshift or temporary. The same word has two very different identities because they come from two different roots.

"Jury," as in makeshift, has a colorful origin. First off, this "jury's" most recent ancestor is an Old French word, "ajurie," which means "help or relief." Some sources disagree and suggest that "jury" is a corruption of the French word for "day," ("jour") which indicates something "juried" is meant to be temporary.

The adjective is nautical. A "jury mast" was a makeshift mast— the "pole" that holds up a ship's sails—fashioned when a storm at sea, or some other calamity, caused the original mast to break. Thus, this new mast came to the aid of the sailors, but it also was meant to be a temporary fix.

The term "jury-rig" still exists, but "jury" as an adjective in isolation has fallen into disuse. Thus, the only "jury" today is the type that you'll find in a courtroom.

Jury, as in group that makes a verdict, comes from root words that mean, variously, oath, swear, and law. A jury swears an oath to uphold the law. The word's most recent ancestor is the Old French "juree."

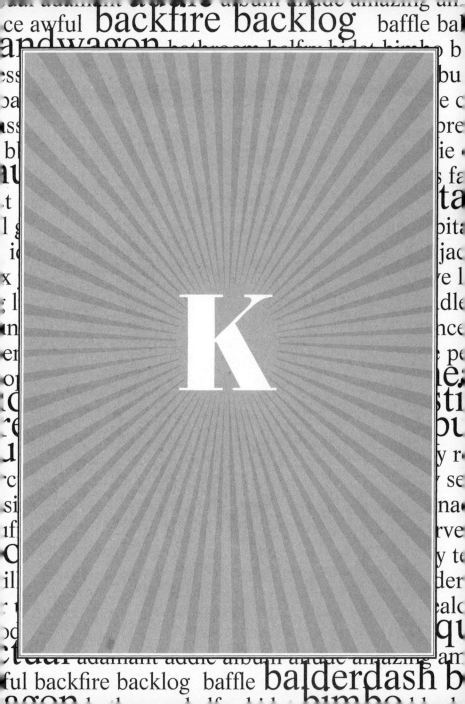

keister

ORIGINAL DEFINITION: strongbox; chest
NEW DEFINITION: buttocks

The English language has thieves and pickpockets to thank for this colorful word for "ass."

The word derives from the German word "kist," meaning chest, as in "place for valuables." Germans kept their loot in their "kists," and, of course, some nefarious folks would break into those "kists."

When English speakers "stole" the word, a chest, safe, or strongbox became a "keister." Thus, a burglar might rifle around in your "keister," looking for nuggets. Enter pickpockets.

By the nineteenth century, pickpockets were so common in England that they make regular appearances in Charles Dickens's work. The charming albeit cheeky Artful Dodger of *Oliver Twist* is a pickpocket, for example.

Since "keister" already referred to a place for valuables, some pickpockets began to call a mark's rear pants pocket a "keister." Thus, "keister" stopped being the pocket and became the fleshy appurtenances underneath the pocket.

ketchup

ORIGINAL DEFINITION: Chinese condiment made of the brine of pickled fish
NEW DEFINITION: tomato-based condiment

For such a quotidian item, ketchup has an exotic history. The Chinese words from which ketchup derived—kichap and koechiap—meant brine of pickled fish. This nasty-sounding concoction, invented by the Chinese in the late 1600s, was intended as a condiment.

Ketchup was common in England by the 1740s, but, at that time, it was used generically to refer to "spiced sauce" and could contain nearly everything: mushrooms, walnuts, shellfish. A tomato-based version was in existence by the early 1800s, but that variety did not become synonymous with the ketchup everyone knows today until the mid-1800s.

One reason tomato ketchup became popular was that many were afraid to eat fresh tomatoes during that time. They were still somewhat exotic, and people thought they might be poisonous, in the same way that people tend to be wary of mushrooms. Folks thought that a processed product like ketchup was safer. Heinz released its version of tomato ketchup in 1876, and the condiment was on its way to tables across America.

By the way, the alternate spelling of "catsup" was an attempt to Anglicize the word ketchup, which people considered too exotic. To this day, both spellings are common.

—— *Fifty-Seven Varieties* ——

For many, ketchup and Heinz are linked. Since 1896, the Pittsburgh company has used as one of its slogans, "57 varieties." Many believe this is the number of products the company offered when it developed the slogan, but they are wrong.

When the company came up with the slogan, it already offered more than sixty products, including mock turtle soup, mincemeat, Indian relish, and even breakfast cereal. One day, company founder Henry J. Heinz saw an ad for a store that offered twenty-one varieties of shoes.

He wanted to create a slogan that was even more impressive. Heinz focused on fifty-seven because five was his lucky number, and seven was his wife's lucky number.

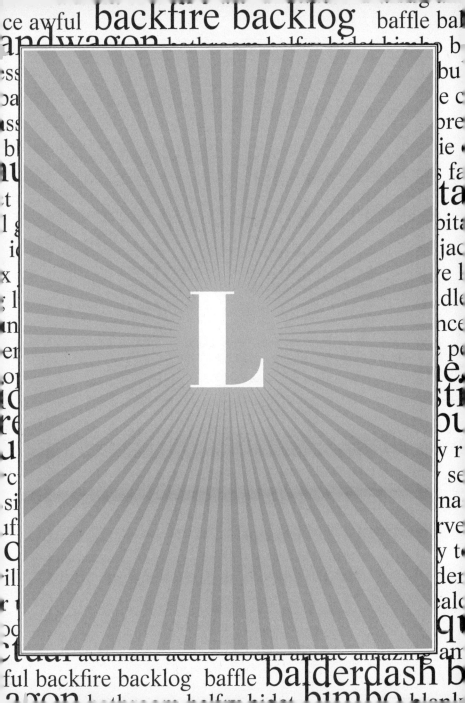

lewd

ORIGINAL DEFINITION: lay (as in, not a member of the clergy)
NEW DEFINITION: lascivious; lecherous

Class distinctions sometimes affect innocent words. Take "lewd," for example. The word meant "nonclerical," as in, this "lewd" person is not a priest or bishop; he's a regular guy. In olden times, members of the clergy were well educated. After all, they needed not only knowledge of God and the Bible but also different ways to refute arguments against God and the Word of God. They needed to be able to parse biblical concordances with the care of a present-day lawyer reading lewd (in the modern sense) text messages from a man to his mistress.

The word degenerated due to snobbery. Someone "nonclerical" is likely to be unlettered . . . i.e., uneducated. Uneducated people—sniff, sniff—were considered coarse and vulgar. Now, one tends to think of "lewd" as connected to its evil twin, "lascivious." It's a word that describes pornography and the stares of dirty old men.

lobby

ORIGINAL DEFINITION: covered walkway
NEW DEFINITION: to attempt to influence the vote of a public official

Long ago, a lobby was a covered walkway, especially one that led to a monastery. The word comes from German and Latin words meaning "home" or "shelter made out of foliage."

By the seventeenth century, "lobby" more commonly was used to describe the entrance hall of a large building. It was the sort of place where people gathered before heading to various offices.

The British House of Commons had such a large lobby. Influence peddlers would teem there like termites in rotten wood. Thus, the people who hung out in lobbies waiting for politicians were said to be "lobbying." A noun became a verb, and foliage transformed into corporate toadies. America, the country that has made lobbying an art form, developed the word "lobbyist" in the 1860s.

lovemaking/making love

ORIGINAL DEFINITION: to pay amorous attention to
NEW DEFINITION: to have sex with

For about 400 years, the word "lovemaking" and the phrase "making love" were equivalent to the modern term "flirting." Modern readers might be nonplussed, for example, when reading the works of F. Scott Fitzgerald. The Jazz Age writer's stories are filled with men and women "making love" at parties and in other conspicuous places. Viewers of the Christmas classic *It's a Wonderful Life* may blanch when innocent, virginal Mary Hatch tells her mom that George Bailey is "making violent love" to her on the couch downstairs.

By the middle of the twentieth century, "lovemaking" began to shift into a more, um, explicit sense. Most likely, that was because the 1950s were a fairly prudish time, and the decade required euphemisms for "having sex."

Some linguists suggest that the change is related to the 1960s hippie mantra "make love, not war." Hippies were known for free love, so if they said "make love," they must have meant "go at it vigorously."

L

—— *Don't Make Love to Us!* ——

Alice Reighly was sick of "cake eaters" (flirtatious men of leisure) ogling her, whistling at her from their automobiles, and attempting to "make love" to her on the streets. As a result, she organized the Anti-Flirt Club in February of 1923.

The club had rules designed to keep young ladies from encouraging this type of man. One was, "Don't wink—a flutter of one eye may cause a tear in the other." Another was, "Don't use your eyes for ogling—they were made for worthier purposes." And, finally, consider, "Don't fall for the slick, dandified cake eater—the unpolished gold of a real man is worth more than the gloss of a lounge lizard."

ludicrous

ORIGINAL DEFINITION: pertaining to play or sport
NEW DEFINITION: ridiculous to the point of being funny

The original Latin word that gave rise to "ludicrous" meant game or play. For the sake of argument, assume that ancient Romans played tiddlywinks and Twister at home and ran footraces outdoors. These, therefore, were "ludicrous" pursuits. Later, the Latin word transformed in meaning to denote "something that amuses." While it's true that games are amusements, so are jokes and tricks.

By the time "ludicrous" entered English, sometime in the early 1600s, it shifted back to meaning "having to do with sport." Thus, jousting was "ludicrous."

As the 1700s ended, however, "ludicrous" made another shift, re-emphasizing "something that amuses." In fact, it took that concept to an extreme. Since the early 1800s, "ludicrous" has meant "excessively ridiculous." One connection is that, when someone says something ludicrous, it's as though he or she is playing a game with you.

---

luxury

ORIGINAL DEFINITION: sexual intercourse (principally for the "not fun" purpose of procreation)
NEW DEFINITION: something unnecessary that makes life more pleasurable

If you haven't had it in a while, then sex may feel like a luxury. You don't *need* it, but it sure would be nice to have. During the Middle Ages, sex literally was a "luxury." The words were synonyms.

The connection was in the word's roots, which suggest excessive or sinful self-indulgence. For thousands of years, the purpose of sex was for procreation within a marriage. It wasn't for fun, and it certainly wasn't for unmarried couples (or for adulterers or for same-sex partners).

Despite all the abjurations against it, love has always been made "inappropriately." That's likely why the word stopped having a negative tone as early as the seventeenth century. At that point, "luxury" began to refer to goods, rather than to people having sex. There was still a sense of self-indulgence that accompanied luxury items, but then, as now, folks (who weren't Puritans, that is) weren't too bothered by self-indulgence.

By the late eighteenth century, luxury came to mean a certain level of excess—like today, when it refers to cable television, DVR, unlimited texting, and steak every weekend. Though, for some lonely folks, sex remains a luxury.

L

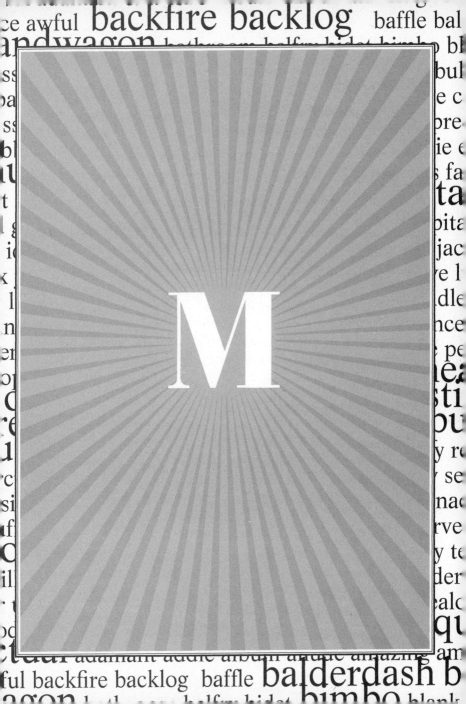

manufacture

ORIGINAL DEFINITION: to make, as goods, by hand
NEW DEFINITION: to mass-produce goods on a machine

If you look at the word manufacture, it suggests that something is made ("fac") by hand ("manu"). And for part of the Middle Ages, that's just what "manufacture" meant. A skilled artisan would "manufacture" goods, possibly with the help of apprentices.

Even before the industrial revolution, which began around 1750, machines began to replace human beings during part of the manufacturing process. As more and more machines "came online," handcrafted goods became ever scarcer.

Since "manufacture" already meant "to produce stuff," it was an easy lexical leap to refer to mass-produced items as being "manufactured." After all, someone had to operate the machines, and some parts of the manufacturing process probably were still done by hand well into the modern era.

Nonetheless, for hundreds of years, "manufacture" has been synonymous with "mass-produced," and goods made entirely by hand are as rare as skilled artisans.

M

---

meddle

ORIGINAL DEFINITION: to mix; mingle
NEW DEFINITION: to interfere in someone else's business

"Meddle" wasn't always a negative word. Until the late 1300s, "meddle" was a synonym for "mix." You would "meddle" the ingredients of a stew. You would "meddle" with friends . . . as in, intermingle with them. You'd "meddle" paints to get a new color.

"Meddle" first got a bad name—or at least an impolite one—starting in the late 1300s. For the next 300 years, people used "meddle" as a euphemism for sexual intercourse: "Did you hear? Bob is meddling Jackie."

As "meddle" fell into the gutter, it gained a negative connotation. When it wasn't being used to describe extramarital affairs, it still suggested "mixing"—but "mixing" where one wasn't welcome. Thus, by the 1400s, "meddle" was pejorative. The word "meddler," used to describe someone like Gladys Kravitz—the quintessential meddler from the TV series *Bewitched*—arrived later that century.

---

minion

ORIGINAL DEFINITION: a favorite
NEW DEFINITION: a sycophant

When "minion" was born, it did not have a pejorative ring. It suggested someone who was a follower, yes, but he or she was not hated by others. A "minion" was a king's favorite subject, a business owner's favorite employee. Others, on the outside, might have looked up to someone else's "minions." The word, after all, has roots that mean: tender, love, and memory. A "minion" was someone you thought well of, in other words.

By the eighteenth century, however, "minion" began to gain its current, negative ring. In light of democracy and self-realization, "minions" became known for their slavish conformity to someone else. In addition, simple jealousy played a part in the word's transformation. No one ever likes the teacher's pet, right?

Nowadays, that's the association one is likely to make with "minions." You might speak of your boss's minions, for example, when you're thinking about those servile sycophants who chase around the Big Kahuna like little, hungry puppies. And where would a bad guy be without his minions? While he masterminds

M

the overthrow of the world—or at least Gotham City—his "little people" can flit about causing various forms of mayhem and chaos.

—— Henchmen vs. Evil Minions ——

Bad guys need either evil minions or henchmen. As noted, "minion" wasn't always a negative word. Neither was "henchman."

Originally, a henchman was a horse groom, someone who took care of a wealthy man's horses. "Hench" is an Old English word via German that means "horse." The word fell out of favor by the seventeenth century, but it was revived by Scottish novelist Sir Walter Scott. Scott believed "henchmen" suggested a man who stands at his master's "haunches," i.e., someone ready at a moment's notice to leap to his defense.

Scott's use of the word, which suggested sycophantic qualities, led to the modern sense of a henchman as someone who does the bidding of a bad guy.

M

miscreant

ORIGINAL DEFINITION: infidel

NEW DEFINITION: unscrupulous person; ne'er-do-well

Initially, being a "miscreant" could get you killed or at least tortured to the point at which death would have been welcome.

During the Crusades (a war fought among Christians, Jews, and Muslims between 1095 and 1274), Christian knights went in search of "miscreants." To them, the word meant, literally, "not believing," as in, someone who does not profess the Christian faith. God himself is the only one who knows how many "miscreants" were killed, maimed, spindled, or mutilated during that period.

Over time, the word "miscreant" softened. By the time Edmund Spenser used it in the late sixteenth century, the word simply meant villain or unscrupulous person. The religious element had all but disappeared.

Nowadays, a miscreant is simply a juvenile delinquent, someone who shoplifts, or someone who has a drawer full of parking tickets. Basically, he or she has done something wrong but is not diabolical. There's a chance that he or she can be reformed before it's too late.

---

mogul

ORIGINAL DEFINITION: Mongol emperor
NEW DEFINITION: rich, powerful person

A nomadic group of central Asians called the Mongols, led by Genghis Khan, conquered China and much of Asia in the early decades of the thirteenth century. In what we now call the Middle East, the Mongols effectively committed genocide, killing up to three-fourths of the region's men, women, and children. Iran's population didn't reach pre-Mongol levels again until the twentieth century! In short, these were powerful (and not very nice) guys.

Gradually, the Mongols lost some of their power. But then they were rallied by Tamerlane (also known as Timur), who served as the inspiration for Shakespeare-contemporary Christopher Marlowe's *Tamburlaine the Great*. Tamerlane died, and once again, it looked like the Mongol empire was over.

Then, in 1526, a descendant of Tamerlane named Babar (or Barbur) invaded and conquered portions of India, calling it the Mogul Empire. "Mogul" was from a Persian word for the Mongols.

M

The Moguls stayed in control of India well into the nineteenth century. Even after they were just figureheads, Mogul emperors made tons of money thanks to British trading throughout India. Thus, "mogul" (with a lowercase "m") came to mean any rich, powerful individual.

——— *Another Mogul* ———

The type of mogul one finds in skiing comes from a completely different root. It comes from Norwegian and German words that mean heap or mound.

moron

ORIGINAL DEFINITION: official designation for an adult with a mental age of eight to twelve years old

NEW DEFINITION: generic insult for someone acting foolishly

No one wants to be called a moron. It's an insult used on playgrounds everywhere. At one time, however, it was the serious, "scientific" term for someone with mild mental disabilities.

The word was coined in 1910 and is based on a Greek word meaning dull. A "moron" was more developed mentally than an imbecile (IQ of 26 to 50; see entry for "imbecile") or an idiot (IQ of 0 to 25; see entry for "idiot"). All these terms were popularized by the also incredibly non-PC-to-today's-ears American Association for the Study of the Feeble-Minded.

As early as the 1920s, the word stopped being technical and became a generic insult to someone's intelligence. If you're called a moron, then you're probably a person of "normal" intelligence who is making an extremely poor choice. Of course, now that people can gain Internet "fame" by being filmed making extremely poor choices, "moronic" behavior is "de rigueur."

---

munition(s)

ORIGINAL DEFINITION: fortification
NEW DEFINITION: weaponry (usually plural)

The roots of the word "munition" suggest walls and fortifications. Soldiers built "munitions" to keep enemies out. They used them for protection, and they used them as a launching pad for various weapons. "Munition" first began to appear in writing in the mid-fifteenth century, and it referred only to walls and fortifications at that time.

Over the next hundred years, in a metonymic shift, soldiers began to associate "munition" primarily with their weaponry store-houses. (Metonymy occurs when one object or concept is used to refer to another closely related object or concept. For example, "the Roosevelt White House" means "Roosevelt's presidency.") Thus, "munitions" became weapons.

About the same time English speakers turned fortifications into weaponry, French soldiers mistakenly made "la munition" into "l'ammunition." The mistake likely was influenced by the French word, "amonition," which means warning.

"Ammunition" spread into English and split from "munitions." "Ammunition" refers specifically to bullets, while "munitions" include everything: cannons, guns, rifles, bullets, etc.

M

nabob

ORIGINAL DEFINITION: deputy governor in Mogul Empire
NEW DEFINITION: someone of great wealth and importance

The late political columnist William Safire once was a speech-writer for Vice President Spiro Agnew. In that capacity, he penned Agnew's most-remembered phrase, "nattering nabobs of negativism." Folks who ran to their dictionaries learned that a "nabob" is a person of great wealth and importance. But before that, a nabob was a very *specific* person of wealth and importance.

The Mogul Empire (see entry for "mogul") controlled most of the Indian subcontinent during the seventeenth and eighteenth centuries. The Moguls controlled so much that they required many deputy governors to look out for the empire's interests.

These deputy governors were called "nawabs," which English speakers transformed into "nabobs." These government officials practiced the time-honored tradition of using their positions to line their own pockets. Thus, they became extremely wealthy and important.

When the British East India Company began to wrestle power away from the Moguls in the late eighteenth century, an English playwright decided the company's directors acted a lot like "nabobs." They made money—often by allegedly illegal means—and wielded tremendous power.

Thus, Samuel Foote wrote a play in 1772 called *The Nabob*, which satirized the British East India Company. The play helped popularize the word "nabob."

N

naughty

ORIGINAL DEFINITION: needy
NEW DEFINITION: disobedient

Originally, "naughty" meant "needy." "Naught" meant (and still means) "nothing," so someone "naughty" had nothing. She was poor. By the 1500s, "naughty" came to mean "vile," "vicious," "just plain bad."

Like "villain" (see entry for "villain"), the word took on this connotation because people of old thought the poor were vile, apparently reasoning, "They wouldn't be poor if they hadn't done something to make God angry, right?!"

Despite those beginnings, "naughty" began to soften in tone. By the middle of the seventeenth century, it became a word most often associated with disobedient children who deserve to wake up to coal-filled stockings on Christmas mornings.

—— *Santa the Stalker* ——

John Frederick Coots and Haven Gillespie aren't household names, but the songwriter and the lyricist, respectively, are responsible for one of the all-time Christmas classics: "Santa Claus Is Coming [sometimes Comin'] to Town."

The song debuted in November 1934 on Eddie Cantor's radio program. By that holiday season, sheet music orders had surpassed 400,000 copies. Hundreds of artists have covered the song, including Bruce Springsteen and Michael Jackson.

Yet, for all the nostalgia the song evokes, its lyrics are just downright creepy: "You better watch out," (!), "You better not cry," (!!) and most frightening of all, "He sees you when you're sleeping." (!!!)

N

nice

ORIGINAL DEFINITION: foolish; stupid
NEW DEFINITION: agreeable; pleasant, as in temperament

This word has traveled more than an international businessperson.

In the fourteenth century, you wouldn't want you or anyone in your family to be called "nice" because it meant that you or those you love were considered extremely dumb. The word's origin is a Latin word meaning "ignorant" or "not knowing."

"Nice" then spent the next 400 or so years adopting and then discarding new meanings. At various times, the word meant timid, fussy, and careful.

By the time the novel became a viable literary form—sometime in the 1700s—the word had solidified to mean agreeable or pleasant or even well-bred.

Of course, "nice" continues to be a pretty elastic word. It can be used sarcastically: "Nice job, idiot." It can be used to show extreme pleasure or approval: "Nice!" And it can be used when you need a generic, "pleasant" word: "What do you think of this flower arrangement, dear?" "Oh, it's nice."

N

nightmare

ORIGINAL DEFINITION: incubus
NEW DEFINITION: distressing dream

Perhaps you've assumed the word "nightmare" has something to do with horses. A mare is a female horse, and nightmares do seem to gallop into one's mind under the cover of darkness. But no. The "mare" in "nightmare" is a word that once meant "incubus."

What's an incubus? She is a female goblin or ogre who flies through your window and lands on your chest. Then, she slowly suffocates you. Isn't that what a nightmare feels like—panic, shortness of breath, suffocation?

People were so convinced that a physical being caused this distress that a "nightmare" was believed literally to be an ogre or goblin until the sixteenth century. After that, most realized that the crushing, suffocating feeling was the emotional reaction to a bad dream.

—— *Nightmares vs. Night Terrors* ——

A night terror differs from a nightmare because of its severity and the fact that night terrors are more likely to affect children than adults. After a night terror, the dreamer often bolts upright and screams. To this day, one synonym for night terror is "incubus attack."

notorious

ORIGINAL DEFINITION: well known
NEW DEFINITION: unfavorably known

From a Latin word meaning "come to know," "notorious" was a synonym for "notable" when it first popped up in writing during the mid-sixteenth century. Thus, royalty might be "notorious" (and not because its various members were busy swimming in the same gene pool or hard at work killing off unwanted ex-wives).

During the 1600s, "notorious" began to take on its pejorative cast, most likely because many famous people were doing bad things. People would refer to notorious smugglers or smut peddlers or crooked politicians. Eventually, the adjective so often referred to negative people and things that it became a negative word, proof of what your parents said about being judged by the company you keep.

—— *Notorious in the Movies* ——

Fans of classic film may associate this word with one of Alfred Hitchcock's first great movies. The 1946 film, *Notorious*, was "notorious" in its day for Hitchcock's creative effort to circumvent the Motion Picture Production Code's attempts to limit onscreen kisses to three seconds.

In the "notorious" scene, Hitchcock shows Cary Grant and Ingrid Bergman kissing for the requisite three seconds, separating lips, nuzzling each other, then diving back to lip-lock land. The scene ultimately lasted almost three minutes and was probably sexier than a simple ten-second kiss might have been.

N

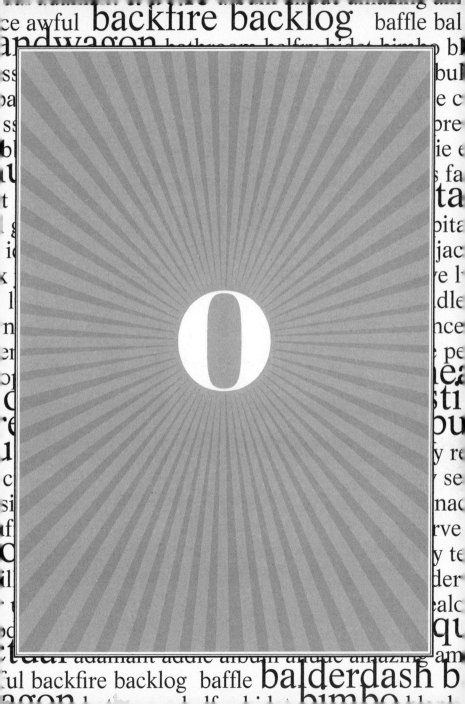

O

obsession

ORIGINAL DEFINITION: act of besieging
NEW DEFINITION: unhealthy fixation

Before it became the purview of stalkers and perverts, "obsession" was a word of war. But first, it took a trip through the paranormal.

The Latin word that gave rise to "obsession" literally means "a besieging." Thus, a warring king would stage an "obsession" at the gates of a rival's castle, for example. Perhaps, even then, a man might focus his interest on a woman to the point that it became a besieging, or an "obsession."

As the Middle Ages gave way to the early modern era, "obsession" became a word akin to "exorcism" (see entry for "exorcise"). With an exorcism, spirits have entered an unfortunate soul's body. During an "obsession," by contrast, an evil spirit stayed "on the outside" but besieged the victim(s) unmercifully.

These meanings of "obsession" aren't too far from the modern concept of a fixation, especially one that's unseemly. The word still suggests a besieging, albeit an internal one, and the adjective that seems most at home in front of "obsession" is "unhealthy." For that matter, sometimes people with obsessions "besiege" those with whom they are obsessed.

---

occupy

ORIGINAL DEFINITION: euphemism for sexual intercourse
NEW DEFINITION: to fill space or time

The word "occupy" has always meant to "fill space and time." But for 300 years or so, "occupy" had an interesting, sexual, chapter in its life.

From the fifteenth through the seventeenth centuries, "occupy" meant to occupy someone sexually. For example, "Did you hear that Robert is occupying the daughter of the yeoman who owns the farm next to his?" During this period, "occupy" also meant, as it always had, to fill in space or time. But it became so associated with sex that people practically stopped using the word.

Eventually, people stopped associating "occupy" with sex, and the word has returned to its original meaning. But you might want to think twice the next time you tell someone you've been "occupying yourself for a while."

OK

ORIGINAL DEFINITION: deliberately misspelled abbreviation for "all correct"; nickname of Martin Van Buren
NEW DEFINITION: all right

For a brief period in the 1830s, Boston newspapers outdid themselves coming up with "humorous" acronyms based on misspellings. Why did this become a fad? You might as well ask why planking became a fad. It just did, that's all.

The *Boston Morning Post* debuted "OK" in its March 23, 1839 edition. It stood for "oll korrect," a "humorous" misspelling of "all correct." But the reason "OK" survived, and many other of these wacky acronyms didn't, is because of Martin Van Buren.

Our not-so-illustrious eighth U.S. president, Martin Van Buren, had the nickname "Old Kinderhook." He was running for re-election not long after the invention of "OK," so the two acronyms got conflated—people began to associate the "oll korrect" type of "OK" with the Martin Van Buren type of "OK." Van Buren

O

lost his re-election bid, by the way. Americans couldn't forgive him for the Panic of 1837 (an ancestor of the Great Depression).

Van Buren wasn't OK, but "OK" was. Before long, people forgot where "OK" came from, stopped using it to refer to Van Buren, and it just became a generic way to say everything's all right.

---

orient

ORIGINAL DEFINITION: to face east
NEW DEFINITION: to find one's bearings; face a certain direction

First came the Orient, that location to which so many European explorers sought an easy all-water passage. Columbus was seeking the Orient when he went in completely the opposite direction and "discovered" North America.

The Orient earned its name because the Latin word at its root means "place where the sun rises." For most Europeans, that direction was east. When Europeans' exploration became widespread, that's the direction most people sought. Thus, the Orient —the area most people today associate with the Middle East and the Far East—was on many people's minds.

By the eighteenth century, "orient" (with a lowercase "o") was a generic term for facing east or designing something to face east. By the nineteenth century, "orient" lost its explicit relationship to the east and suggested facing any specific, desired direction. By extension, it has come to mean finding one's bearings and thus heading in the right direction . . . whichever direction that might be.

—— *Avoid the Oriental* ——

When first used to refer to a specific geographical region, "Oriental" was associated with the Near East, which has been called the Middle East since the first half of the twentieth century. By the nineteenth century, "Oriental" was equivalent to the Far East: Japan, Korea, China, etc.

As the twentieth century progressed, the word "Oriental" fell into disrepute. Why? If Westerners include diverse cultures like Korea, China, and Japan under one umbrella, it's the semantic equivalent of saying, "They all look alike to me." Thus, the term typically is not used today.

O

paraphernalia

ORIGINAL DEFINITION: woman's property, other than her dowry
NEW DEFINITION: assortment of odds and ends

Women don't typically have dowries anymore, but they used to be one of the "advantages" of marriage. If you were a man, you might choose a wife based on her dowry, which was goods—money, farm animals, slaves if you were below the Mason-Dixon Line—a father would give to his new son-in-law.

Anything a woman owned that was not part of her dowry was called "paraphernalia." The root word, "paraphernal," was Latin for just that: stuff a woman owned independent of her dowry. Since women didn't tend to work outside of the house much until the twentieth century, their "paraphernalia" probably didn't amount to much. They probably had some clothing, some childhood mementos, some small items of furniture, etc.

By the close of the eighteenth century, "paraphernalia" stopped being explicitly connected to a woman's property. The word, instead, focused on the fact that much of that property consisted of assorted odds and ends, a mishmash of stuff.

pariah

ORIGINAL MEANING: drummer
NEW MEANING: social outcast

"Pariah" is one of those words—like villain (see entry for "villain")—that comes to the English language via social snobbery.

From an East Indian word meaning "drummer" or "one who drums," early "pariahs" belonged to the Indian labor caste. In other words, "pariahs" were at the very bottom of the social ladder. Actually, they were not even on the first rung. Traditionally, they were field workers. Some of them were employed to beat drums to keep people awake and working hard.

India was effectively a European colony from 1613, when the East India Trading Company was one of the world's largest conglomerates, until 1947. During this time, Europeans often employed members of this "drumming" class as domestics and personal servants.

The British, in power for many of those years, were no strangers to rigid social stratification. They considered these "pariahs" socially inferior. Thus, through the magic of metaphor, "pariah" began to refer to anyone considered a social outcast, regardless of his or her income or station.

pencil

ORIGINAL DEFINITION: paintbrush
NEW DEFINITION: writing instrument containing graphite

One of the "roots" of this word is the Latin "penis," which used to mean "tail" but also always had the meaning of "dangling male appendage."

A later root word meant "brush," and that's what "pencil" meant for most of the Middle Ages. It was a very fine (as in "thin") brush, often made from camel hair, which was used for everyday writing. Then, in 1565, a huge graphite deposit was found in England. Early scientists mistakenly thought it was actually lead.

Someone—surely a millionaire in his day—came up with the bright idea of using the graphite to make sturdy writing utensils that didn't have to be dipped in ink or to rely on the shearing of camels. Thus, by the turn of the seventeenth century, "pencil" began to mean "graphite-containing writing instrument."

P

By the way, the pencil could for many years cause lead poisoning, even though it contained no lead . . . in its writing component. The lead was in the paint used to decorate the pencil.

—— *I Made These Pencils Because* —— *I Wish to Write Deliberately*

Henry David Thoreau is considered by many to be the godfather of the modern ecology movement. He famously spent time in a cabin he built on Walden Pond, in a nineteenth-century version of living off the grid, writing in *Walden* that he "wished to live deliberately."

Yet, Thoreau wasn't just a guy who spent all his spare time dreaming and writing. The pencils you use today are a variation of the type created more than a century ago by this Transcendentalist.

Thoreau's father, John Thoreau, began a pencil business with his brother-in-law after a large deposit of graphite was discovered in New Hampshire. Their pencils sold fairly well, but their quality was poor. Their graphite smeared easily on the page. Something was needed to bind the graphite securely to the wood of the pencil.

Enter Henry David. He figured out that clay would work perfectly as a binder. After that, their pencils wrote flawlessly and sold well. But Thoreau refused to make any money from his discovery.

---

penthouse

ORIGINAL DEFINITION: humble building with a sloped roof attached to a larger building

NEW DEFINITION: swanky apartment on the top floor of a building

Contrary to popular belief, Jesus probably was born in a "penthouse." Not a swanky urban penthouse, mind you, but a simple, humble dwelling with a sloped roof. After all, that's the original definition for a penthouse.

The modern sense of "penthouse" began to appear in the 1920s, a time of great change and rapid expansion in American history. "Skyscrapers" were being built, and the apartments often placed at their pinnacles were called "penthouses." After all, they were still "attached" to larger buildings.

According to the *New York Observer*, the average cost of a New York City apartment in 2010—not even a penthouse, mind you— was $1.43 million. For most, you'd need more money than God in order to let your children be born in a penthouse. Penthouses have come a long way from their humble beginnings. . . .

peruse

ORIGINAL DEFINITION: to use up; wear out
NEW DEFINITION: to read carefully

First, let's clear up a misconception about this word. For some reason, many people today believe "peruse" means to skim or scan a passage quickly. In fact, it means the opposite, and for proof, you can look at the word's original meaning.

During the fourteenth century, "peruse" referred to something one had paid so much attention to, or used so much, that it was now almost useless. For example, you used a feedbag so much that it developed numerous holes and was no longer useful on the farm. For that matter, a horse may have been "perused" because it had been worked to near death.

By the 1500s, "peruse" began to refer to reading something carefully, in effect, to "wear out" a text by reading it closely or

P

repeatedly. The shift makes sense when one considers that the Gutenberg press first printed a book in 1456.

After that invention, more and more people owned Bibles (among other works), and many "perused" their Bibles carefully to make sure they were doing right . . . or, more likely, to prove that their neighbors were doing wrong. Things haven't changed *that* much in 500 years.

photogenic

ORIGINAL DEFINITION: producing light
NEW DEFINITION: looking good in photographs

Initially, the word "photogenic" was coined to describe what everyone now calls photography. "Photo" means "light," and "genic" means "produces." In biology class, you might learn about photogenic bacteria, which means they generate light. Likewise, early efforts at photographs were called "photogenic drawings." They were pictures made, in a sense, out of light.

Well, the American version of English always has believed brevity is the soul of wit. Or maybe Americans are just lazy. Regardless, it didn't take long before "photogenic drawings" begot "photographs" which begot "photos."

"Photogenic" changed its principal meaning and began to describe someone who "takes good pictures" as Hollywood begot the nation's first superstar feeding frenzy. If you think about it, you could say that these "stars" shine . . . just like a photogenic, light-generating bacterium. And since most stars look good in pictures, the word took on that meaning.

P

pineapple

ORIGINAL DEFINITION: a pinecone
NEW DEFINITION: a tropical fruit

An "apple" was once a generic word for "fruit." Considering that, the original definition of "pineapple" makes sense. Pine trees drop their "fruit" on the ground, and these "pineapples" grow new pine trees. Around 1700, some scientists began to call these spiny objects "pinecones" because of their shape.

There might have been another reason for this semantic shift. European exploration was going strong in the mid-seventeenth century. Explorers found a tropical fruit that resembled "pineapples"— i.e., pinecones—so explorers took to calling them "pineapples."

As two different kinds of "pineapples" became common, confusion ensued. Thus, by the eighteenth century, pineapples were pineapples, and pinecones were pinecones.

—— *Hawaiian Fruit?* ——

Even though you probably associate pineapples with Hawaii, they are not native to the islands. Pineapples originate in South America, and some historians credit their European discovery to Christopher Columbus himself.

An explorer—it's unclear which one—introduced the pineapple to Hawaii in the sixteenth century. In the 1880s, Captain John Kidwell became the first to cultivate the pineapple on a large scale, but his pineapple plantation soon was dwarfed by that of industrialist James Dole, whose name remains associated with pineapples to this day.

P

pioneer

ORIGINAL MEANING: foot soldier
NEW DEFINITION: one who leads the way; one who does something first

For centuries, a "pioneer" was a foot soldier. He was a grunt, nameless, expendable. He basically performed reconnaissance missions, striking out a little ahead of the rest of the army, making sure all was clear before going back to get everyone else. If he got blown up, chopped into pieces, or crushed by a booby trap, then that was too bad. At least no one "important" got hurt.

Eventually, people realized the bravery that it took to be a "pioneer." After all, these guys (and they would have been guys) went into uncharted territory that was fraught with peril. Sure, they were ordered to go and would have been court-martialed if they didn't, but pioneers exhibited valor nonetheless.

As the Age of Discovery (fifteenth to seventeenth centuries) took root, pioneers blossomed. These explorers, no longer anonymous, became famous, lending their European names to land masses and bodies of water inhabited by (newly expendable) indigenous people.

To this day, "pioneer" has something of a heroic ring to it.

---

poll

ORIGINAL MEANING: head; hair
NEW MEANING: survey

Polling has become the lifeblood of American politicians, and polls are as omnipresent as hair on one's head. That makes sense, as it turns out.

During medieval times, "poll" was a noun that meant the "top of the head," or "hair." Thus one would get one's "poll" cut.

At the dawn of the modern era, "poll" began to gain its political association. When a vote was taken, sometimes a "head count" was used. The "poll"—in its original sense—was the part that a public official could see and count in order to register votes. Thus, "polling" came to mean counting votes related to a particular issue or candidate.

The word made a slight shift in 1824, when a "straw poll" was used by a Pennsylvania newspaper to determine the likely winner of the presidential race between Andrew Jackson and John Quincy Adams. The poll, a survey of voters' likely ballot choice, accurately predicted Jackson would win the election.

When George Gallup brought statistics to polling in 1936, he helped transform the most common modern concept of polling from counting votes to include gathering information about public opinions.

---

prestige

ORIGINAL DEFINITION: trick; illusion; deception
NEW DEFINITION: the quality of being esteemed by others

"Prestige" used to mean "trick." Yes, as in something a magician performs, but also as in "deception." "Prestige" suggested that you intentionally misled someone. You dazzled him into believing your story and then took him for everything he was worth.

The sense of "dazzling" others led "prestige" to undergo a transformation. Some posit that the word first was used with a positive connotation to describe Napoleon, who not only was

P

esteemed but was also quite tricky. He seems to have embodied both the old and new meanings of "prestige."

By the close of the nineteenth century, "prestige" became the wholly positive word the English language knows today. If you dazzle someone with your prestige, then you haven't tricked her. You've impressed her with your abilities. People tend to admire those who attend prestigious universities or get published in prestigious journals. A woman of prestige is one whom everyone admires for the content of her character.

pretty

ORIGINAL DEFINITION: cunning
NEW DEFINITION: attractive

"Pretty" has had a rather byzantine life. Its meaning shifted substantially between Old English and Middle English, and for a good portion of its life, "pretty" was a word used to describe men, not women.

The Old English word that led to "pretty" meant "cunning" and "artful." Someone who "pulled one over on you" was guilty of a "pretty" trick, for example. By the fifteenth century, however, "pretty" became synonymous with "manly" and "gallant." Most likely, the Old English word and a similar word from another language got intermingled. This was a common occurrence in the early history of the English language.

Once "pretty" became "manly," its meaning shifted again, to "attractive." This must be when the word "switched genders" because then, as now, a lot of men don't want to be complimented for their looks because they think it's "unmanly."

By the mid-fifteenth century, "pretty" took on its current meaning of "attractive" . . . but not really "beautiful." Perhaps this ambivalence is what caused people in the sixteenth century to begin using "pretty" as a modifier, as in "pretty plow." This version of "pretty" seems in keeping with something that's not ugly, not beautiful, but in between.

promiscuous

ORIGINAL DEFINITION: consisting of a garbled-up mixture of people or things

NEW DEFINITION: characterized by having many sexual partners

When Shakespeare was constructing his masterful tragedies, "promiscuous" was a completely nonsexual word that might have described a big mess. For example, the seventeenth-century version of a hoarder might have had a "promiscuous" collection of odds and ends filling up every nook and cranny of his hovel. Or a street fair would have collected a "promiscuous" group of men, women, and children.

Given that any indiscriminate mixture of people just begs for potential scandals, wagging tongues, and sideways glances, it's not surprising that the word began to mean "someone who is indiscriminate in his or her sexual partners." That definition didn't become widespread until the turn of the twentieth century, though.

P

quaint

ORIGINAL DEFINITION: cunning; artfully contrived; meticulous
NEW DEFINITION: pleasingly old-fashioned

Q

"Quaint" harks back to the same Latin word that gave the English language "cognizant." It's a short jump from cognizance to craftiness. If you're cognizant, you're aware of all the angles, and you can be cunning and crafty. Thus, around the thirteenth century, this was "quaint's" meaning.

About 100 years later, "quaint" grew a new limb and came to mean "cleverly made" or "artfully contrived," as in a "quaint lie." The shift is reasonable. If you're cunning, you'll make up stories to get what you want.

By the fifteenth century, "quaint" meant meticulous or fastidious. The semantic shift here is a little more of a stretch, but most likely it comes from the sense of someone being very careful in covering his tracks after he's told many "artfully contrived" stories. You can't be too careful; someone might catch you in a lie.

By the turn of the nineteenth century, "quaint" put on a new, artfully contrived, definition. It basically picked up bits and pieces of its earlier meanings and fashioned a new denotation out of them: pleasingly old-fashioned.

There is a certain "fussy" quality to the modern version of the word, which calls to mind "fastidiousness." And there is a sense that today, something "quaint" is clever, distinctive, or unusual, harkening back to its original meaning.

Q

—— Chaucer's "Quaint" ——

The most unusual use of "quaint" is by Geoffrey Chaucer, author of *The Canterbury Tales*. In his bawdy "Miller's Tale," the word means "cunt." Since one of "quaint's" lesser meanings, then as now, is "unusual" or "different," Chaucer seems to have used the word the way he did because a woman's intimate anatomy is so different from that of a man's.

One way or the other, the earthy miller who tells the story is inordinately fond of the word. The story is all about people cuckolding each other in artfully contrived ways, so the story demonstrates more than one meaning of quaint.

qualm

ORIGINAL DEFINITION: disaster; death; utter destruction
NEW DEFINITION: slight pang of conscience

What a difference a few centuries make! In its earliest incarnation, a "qualm" was a terrible thing indeed. It meant, variously, kill, die, plague, and utter destruction. If a "qualm" visited your family, you'd be lucky if there were any survivors.

By the early sixteenth century, "qualm" relaxed its death grip to become "a feeling of faintness." The most likely reason for the connection was that if you're near death, you'll feel faint. By the middle of that century, "qualm" meant "a feeling of uneasiness." If you're facing utter destruction, then you'll certainly feel at least uneasy.

Finally, by the mid-seventeenth century, "qualm" began to take on its familiar, modern meaning of a prick in one's conscience. Certainly, if you have qualms, you feel uneasy. You might even feel faint.

quarantine

ORIGINAL DEFINITION: a specific period of forty days
NEW DEFINITION: act of placing sick people in isolation in order not to spread disease

If you are a Christian and a churchgoer (or were forced to go to Sunday school as a kid), then you probably remember the story of Christ's temptation in the desert. Remember? Just before he began his active ministry, he isolated himself in the desert for a period of time, often designated as forty days. During that time, Satan tempted him to leave behind his ministry and give in to worldly temptations.

Historically, "quarantine" is the name of the desert in which Christ endured Satan's temptations, although the word also, basically, means "forty" since it's a variation of the more familiar "quad." So it's mighty convenient that the name of the desert also is the name of the period of time Jesus spent there.

Go forward 1,000 years or so, and "quarantine" became a period of forty days during which a widow could lay claim to her deceased husband's property. Add another century or two, and you'll find yourself in the era of exploration. During this period, if a ship was believed to be carrying disease, it was "quarantined" off the coast for—you guessed it—forty days. Eventually, the word dropped its association with the "forty" that actually is part of its root, but retained its meaning of keeping ill people isolated in order not to spread disease.

R

recalcitrant

ORIGINAL DEFINITION: to kick back (as a mule or horse)
NEW DEFINITION: stubborn; resistant to authority

If you're a word nerd, you may have pondered "recalcitrant." It seems to have a root related to "calcite," which is a family of rocks that includes limestone and marble. These are very heavy substances. They are resistant to movement. Thus, you may have thought "recalcitrant" is a word that, metaphorically, touches on the heaviness of calcite.

But you'd be wrong. The word is metaphorical, but its roots aren't in the mineral kingdom. They're in the animal kingdom.

The word's Latin roots suggest a horse kicking back at its owner because it is injured or because it is simply being stubborn. When "recalcitrant" (literally "to kick back") first entered English, it still suggested an animal kicking back toward its owner.

It's not a metaphorical leap to take this image of a horse or mule kicking at its owner and transfer it to people who act stubborn. By the nineteenth century, mules and horses no longer played any part in "recalcitrant." It had become simply a synonym for stubborn.

relay

ORIGINAL DEFINITION: hunting term meaning fresh pack of hounds
NEW DEFINITION: race in which a series of runners carries a handed-off baton

Long before it was a word associated with track and field events, "relay" was associated with the upper-crust sport of fox hunting.

During the fifteenth century, a "relay" worked something like the following: You and your hounds are chasing a fox through the woods in a certain direction. Eventually, your dogs tire and lose the scent of the fox. Thus, you keep a reserve pack of hounds at a certain distance from your starting point, and let the fresh pack take over when the original hounds have exhausted themselves.

You can see how this is related to the modern-day relay race, in which lead runners hold a baton, sprint at top speed for a certain distance, and hand the baton to another runner, who runs a predetermined distance before handing off the baton, and so on. "Fresh" runners take the place of "exhausted" runners. Yet, the expression "relay race" didn't become common until the turn of the twentieth century.

rigmarole

ORIGINAL DEFINITION: list; catalogue
NEW DEFINITION: nonsense; busywork

One popular game in the Middle Ages was called Ragman roll, Ragman's roll, Rageman, or Ragman. Basically, the game required people to pull one of several strings attached to a line of verses about a different character. Then, the player would read the humorous and insulting verse about that character, which also was supposed to describe the player himself.

The game's name got garbled into "rigmarole," which at first meant list or catalogue. This meaning was related to the list of verses one could choose from during the game. Eventually, the word gained a negative connotation and suggested rambling, nonsensical speech or writing.

The word gained another meaning during the twentieth century. It began to be used to describe school-related or job-related tasks that seemed designed simply to make people do more work than necessary in order to keep them busy. Enough with the rigmarole! It takes time away from students' and employees' busy texting-while-on-the-clock schedule!

R

— *Nonsense 'R' Us* —

For some reason, English has many fun and interesting synonyms for "nonsense." Of course, life often is filled with nonsense, so maybe that's why so many words are needed for it.

Synonyms of "rigmarole" include: babble, balderdash (see entry for "balderdash"), baloney, blather, bull, bunk, drivel, foolishness, gibberish, gobbledygook, hogwash, palaver, poppycock, prattle, rubbish, and trash.

But consider for a moment one of the newer words on the list: "gobbledygook." The word was coined in 1944 by a member of the U.S. House of Representatives. Rep. Maury Maverick (D-TX) coined "gobbledygook" in response to government's already common use of euphemisms for starting war, such as "activation" or "implementation."

Maverick said the word was supposed to mimic the sound a turkey makes. By the way, he was descended from the "Maverick" who didn't brand his cattle and thus gave rise to the word maverick, which means "one who doesn't follow the rules."

---

rosary

ORIGINAL DEFINITION: rose garden
NEW DEFINITION: formal Catholic prayer cycle; beaded necklace used to help recite the prayer cycle

During medieval times, a "rosary" was a rose garden. While most who lived during this time endured abject misery—malnutrition, disease, stillbirths, early deaths—some must have had the leisure time necessary to walk about in formal gardens.

When they weren't in gardens, they were in church. And in those days, that meant the Roman Catholic Church. As people died, lords and ladies recited formal prayer cycles focusing on five sacred mysteries, i.e., sacred miracles. As an aid to remembering the cycle, worshipers used a circle of prayer beads.

Over time, the faithful began to compare the cycle of prayers to a "rosary" because, metaphorically, the cycle was a "garden of prayers" out of which grew spiritual comfort and the promise of heaven. By the seventeenth century, "rosary" came to denote the chain of prayer beads as well.

R

---

rubber

ORIGINAL DEFINITION: thing that rubs
NEW DEFINITION: elastic material

For centuries, a "rubber" was just what it sounds like. It was something (or someone?) that "rubbed." Thread in your pantaloons irritating your legs? That was a rubber.

When pencils came along (in the mid-sixteenth century; see entry for "pencil"), erasers were called rubbers. That's what erasers did. They rubbed out stray marks and unwanted words.

It took a French explorer and geographer to make "rubber" the substance the world finds in everything from tires to, well, rubbers (as in prophylactics). Charles Marie de la Condamine of France lived during the eighteenth century. He spent a lot of time in Ecuador studying the equator (seriously). While there, he also became the first Westerner to encounter what is now known as rubber.

Condamine brought the substance back home to France. Since it initially was used as an eraser, people took to calling the substance "rubber." The name stuck. Calling a condom a rubber, by the way, began in the 1920s or 1930s.

R

S

sad

ORIGINAL DEFINITION: satisfied; satiated
NEW DEFINITION: sorrowful

The English language has jaded fourteenth-century lords and ladies enduring the world-weariness of ennui to thank for making "sad" . . . well, sad.

Initially, "sad" meant satisfied, satiated, full, or well-fed. In short, it had all kinds of positive connotations. And it lasted that way from the Old English period well into the Middle English period. For 1,000 years or so, "sad" was happy as a clam.

As "sad" got older, however, people began to focus on the negative side of satisfaction and fulfillment. It would seem that, as Peggy Lee did 700 years later, people began asking, "Is that all there is?"

"Sad" came to mean weary and tired of. If you're fully satiated, then what's left to acquire? Ultimately, by the fourteenth century, "sad" lost all connection to its happier days and became a synonym for "sorrowful," which it remains to this day. How sad!

scamp

ORIGINAL DEFINITION: highwayman; thief
NEW DEFINITION: impish youngster

In the seventeenth century, as now, "scamper" meant to flee. By the mid-eighteenth century, some dialects adopted the curtailed "scamp" and gave it the definition "to roam." By the close of the eighteenth century, "scamp" was used to describe a particular sort who roamed: the dreaded highwayman.

Readers of Dickens are familiar with this character. He lay in wait along roads between London and the hinterlands. When a lone carriage filled with travelers appeared, he sprang into action, helping himself to the valuables of the terrified sojourners.

By the turn of the nineteenth century, "scamp" softened and became a nickname for an impish child. Why? Highwaymen largely were creatures of myth by that time. The railroads were one factor. Passengers were on rails as much as they were in carriages. Executions of highwaymen were another. But the most likely reason for the decline of highwaymen was . . . highway robbery, after a fashion.

England created a series of manned toll roads, which compromised the guerrilla tactics of the highwaymen. Thus, travelers didn't give their valuables to thieves, but they still parted with cash, giving it to the state. So "scamps" are now simply mischievous youths, like Dennis the Menace or Bart Simpson. They're not evil; they're just troublemakers who, deep down inside, have hearts of gold.

S

---

scavenger

ORIGINAL DEFINITION: street sweeper; tax collector
NEW DEFINITION: one who combs through refuse looking for useful items; animals that get sustenance from dead animals

If you've ever compared the IRS to a wake of vultures (yes, a group of vultures is called a wake), then you're not far off the mark.

In its earliest incarnation, a "scavenger" was a street sweeper. His job was to remove refuse from the streets. A few of them may have pocketed items they found as they pushed around their brooms, but that's not what gave rise to the modern concept of scavenger.

For that, the English language has tax collectors to thank. In London, those tasked by the crown with collecting taxes from foreign merchants were called "scavengers." They, literally, combed through someone's earnings and removed a substantial portion. Thus, "scavenger" developed a bad name.

By the sixteenth century, "scavenger" completed its transformation to a mostly pejorative word. Scavengers became people who combed through trash (or visited estate sales) and looked for useful items.

By the seventeenth century, the concept was borrowed for animals such as vultures and buzzards. And by the twentieth century, the word—coming full circle—often was used to refer to tax collectors.

scofflaw

ORIGINAL DEFINITION: one who drinks bootleg or illegal alcohol
NEW DEFINITION: a habitual law-breaker

"Scofflaw" sounds like an ancient word, like one borrowed from Old English. Nope. The word is less than 100 years old, and it's one of the few to which the English language can take credit for coinage.

Actually, English must give credit to two people for this word. A 1923 Boston contest asked folks to submit a word meaning "lawless drinker of illegally made or obtained liquor." (It was during Prohibition, yet many people continued to drink at will.)

Independently of one another (but for the same contest), Henry Dale and Kate Butler coined the word "scofflaw." The word clearly suggests someone who "scoffs" at "laws" he considers stupid, and violations of Prohibition laws were more common-place than speeding tickets.

Despite "scofflaw's" "youth," the word already has shifted from its original meaning. After Prohibition ended, the word "scofflaw" remained. Today, it's no longer connected to alcohol, but it still suggests someone who habitually violates laws she considers petty and insignificant. The word isn't used for serious criminals. Picture, for example, the person whose windshield is a confetti of parking tickets or someone who keeps getting speeding tickets but never stops speeding.

S

—— *Neologisms* ——

Scofflaw is a neologism of relatively recent vintage. A neologism is a word coined by someone or some group that then passes into everyday language. Often, people don't know these words began as neologisms. For example:

- "Chortle" is a combination of "chuckle" and "snort" and was coined by author Lewis Carroll in his poem, "The Hunting of the Snark."
- "Catch-22," which describes a choice with no chance for a positive outcome, was coined by Joseph Heller, and it serves as the title of his best-known novel.
- Science fiction author William Gibson is responsible for giving us the word "cyberspace."
- "Gerrymandering," or rigging political districts to make them benefit one candidate over another, was coined in 1812. It was named for Massachusetts Gov. Elbridge Gerry, who used this tactic. The word is a cross between Gerry's name and salamander, because wags of the day felt the newly created district resembled a salamander.

shifty

ORIGINAL DEFINITION: able to manage on one's own; capable
NEW DEFINITION: using deceptive, dishonest methods to gain success

Shifty lawyers. Shifty bankers. Shifty used car salesmen. Today, those descriptions are insulting. But if you were living in the mid-sixteenth century (and replaced "car" with "cart"), then you would have been complimenting these folks. You would have, in effect, been saying that these are lawyers/bankers/cart salesmen who are capable, who get the job done, and who are responsible and self-motivating.

By the middle of the nineteenth century, "shifty" began to refer almost exclusively to those who would use any means necessary to get ahead.

This shift in "shifty" makes sense. If someone is capable and resourceful, then he will be successful. Sometimes, though, no amount of hard work will lead to success. That's when people "do what they gotta do" to create an anticipated result. In the grand march of life, many have withheld evidence, fudged numbers, or rolled back odometers instead of attaining success through sheer hard work.

—— *The Making of Makeshift* ——

The word "makeshift" came along after "shifty" had completed its negative transformation. At first, it denoted a rogue. Later, it came to describe something put together as a temporary fix.

shrew

ORIGINAL DEFINITION: an evil, spiteful person of either gender
NEW DEFINITION: an evil, spiteful woman

The most famous of all shrews is Katherina Minola. She's a spit-fire, not one to take crap from anyone . . . especially from men. She meets her match in Petruchio, who ultimately "tames" her into a pleasant, docile bride. Since its earliest performances, not everyone has believed "all's well that ends well" in Shakespeare's misogynistic *The Taming of the Shrew.*

S

Two things are clear. For one, "shrew" referred specifically to women by the late sixteenth century, when Shakespeare wrote that play. Originally, it referred to a spiteful person of either sex. And for another, the word is, in fact, based on beliefs about shrews, as in the nocturnal rodents.

Shrews—the animals—were believed to be particularly nasty critters, and there is some truth to the accusation. For one thing, some shrews have a poisonous bite. For another, these are extremely territorial animals that will stop at nothing to drive off rival shrews. They join up with other shrews only to mate and then go back to hating one another.

One thing is *not* clear. Why did "shrew" stop referring to both men *and* women? Most likely it hearkens back to the same misogyny that helped birth Shakespeare's play, once considered a comedy, now often considered insulting to women.

For centuries, men dominated most cultures. They certainly weren't going to allow anyone to refer to *them* as "shrews." Thus, they palmed off the word onto women. Men sometimes are admired for not taking crap, yet many (unflattering) words exist to describe women who do the same.

silly

ORIGINAL DEFINITION: helpless; weak; unsophisticated
NEW DEFINITION: foolish; lacking good sense

"Silly," like "villain" or "clown" (see entries for "clown" and "villain"), is a word that comes to its modern meaning via class warfare, medieval style. Basically, "villain" used to refer to "villagers," whom many thought guilty of all sorts of miscreant (see entry for "miscreant") and perverted behavior. Villains were the Middle Ages's version of rednecks.

"Silly" carries a similar suggestion. The word has changed quite a bit during its lifetime, but for most who lived in the Middle Ages, the word suggested the "helpless" and "unsophisticated." It was used to describe hayseeds who might come into town and be completely bemused (see entry for "amuse") by all the newfangled sights.

People who lived out in the country and didn't have what passed for modern conveniences circa 1550 were called "silly." People who were content to live their lives without having a steady job were called "silly." Ultimately, "silly" came to mean "feeble-minded." The thinking went something like this: "Surely these people who don't contribute to society aren't normal. They must be pitied because they're not right in the head."

Thus, "silly" was a word used to describe people the bourgeoisie considered irresponsible. It still contains that sense, but more often refers to people just being foolish or immature.

siren

ORIGINAL DEFINITION: sea nymph who leads sailors to their doom thanks to her beautiful singing
NEW DEFINITION: loud, piercing sound of warning

In *The Odyssey*, the "sirens" are a group of sea nymphs whose beautiful singing lures sailors to crash their ships onto rocks. The beauty of their voices leads directly to destruction. Odysseus, hero of the epic, decides he wants to hear the sirens' song. He gets his men to tie him to his ship's mast so that he will be unable to pilot the ship toward harm. The men stop up their ears. The image of a bound Odysseus, struggling to steer toward devastation, is one of *The Odyssey's* most enduring.

S

The modern sense of a siren—as a piercing warning sound—didn't emerge until the end of the nineteenth century. As steamboats crowded Mark Twain's mighty Mississippi River, they occasionally needed to send out warning whistles to others. At some point, these warning whistles began to be called sirens. At least there's a "watery" connection between the old and new sirens. Ultimately, the word was used to describe the sound ambulances made as they roared through town.

The irony, of course, is that the original sirens made noise that lured seafarers *to* destruction, while modern sirens make noises designed to keep civilians *safe from* destruction.

slave

ORIGINAL DEFINITION: alternate spelling of Slav
NEW DEFINITION: person owned by another and forced to work for free

Several thousand years ago, in portions of present-day Poland and Russia, lived a group of people who called themselves "slovos." For them, "slovo" meant "word," so they were "the people who speak words."

In Latin, "slovos" ultimately transformed to Slav (and was capitalized). The Slavs were agrarian for the most part, rather than warriors. Thus, they often were conquered by others. At one time or another, seemingly every nation of the medieval world conquered the Slavs, including the Celts, the Huns, and the Goths.

Some of these Slavs finally got wise and began to organize themselves into martial groups that tried their own hands at invasion and conquering. They invaded the Balkans, and they tried to take land away from the Germans.

The Germans, in modern parlance, kicked Slavic ass. The Germans repelled the Slavs from their turf and turned many of them into servants. For the Germans, "slave" was just an alternate spelling of Slav. Thus, "slave" became someone forced to work by another and, by extension, someone owned by another.

---

slur

ORIGINAL DEFINITION: thin mud
NEW DEFINITION: slander; aspersion

The Middle English word from which "slur" originates meant "thin mud." It came from an older word meaning "to track mud in." If you left footprints in your hut after feeding the yaks, then

your wife or mother may have yelled at you for "slurring" the
. . . dirt floor? At least that dirt wasn't wet and slimy before you
messed it up!

As early as the 1600s, the word began to take on its modern
meaning, "to cast aspersions." The shift in meaning is straight-
forwardly metaphoric. "Slur" was mud. Mud stains, smudges, and
dirties things. "Slur's" contemporary meaning suggests people
who use words to dirty, smudge, or stain the reputations of others.

The original sense of the word also is captured in the musical
use of "slur." In music, to slur is to slide over a series of notes without separating them distinctly, much the way someone might slide
over a floor that's covered in thin mud.

S

---

slut

ORIGINAL DEFINITION: a slovenly, untidy person; not exclusively
a woman
NEW DEFINITION: a prostitute; a promiscuous woman

This word did not always exclusively refer to females. In fact, it
originally had no sexual implications at all.

The word derives from another that means "mud," and "slut"
originally was a slovenly, filthy (as in dirty, not as in sexy), dirty
person. Usually the person in question was a woman, but Geoffrey
Chaucer uses the word "sluttish" at times to describe an equally
disheveled man.

Sometime in the fifteenth century, "slut" began to refer specifically to women, and it gained its current sexual denotation. One
cause for the change was that maids sometimes were called "sluts"
because they did a lot of (literally) dirty work, so they wound up

looking dirty. These ladies also were poor and may have done more than laundry to earn their living.

For a time, the word softened in meaning and lost some of its sting because, in the seventeenth century, "slut" actually became a term of endearment for an impish little girl, not unlike the way scamp (see entry for "scamp") became a term of endearment for an impish little boy.

Eventually, "slut" regained its harsh tone but lost its association with literal dirtiness. Instead, the word began to emphasize the metaphorical meaning of "dirty," as in "up for anything, due, possibly, to loose morals."

snack

ORIGINAL DEFINITION: to bite (by a dog)
NEW DEFINITION: something to eat between meals; the act of eating between meals

Too many snacks can make you feel awful because they just add empty calories to your midsection. At one time, "snacks" were even more painful.

The word "snack" derives from an old Dutch word that meant "snatch." When the word jumped to English, around the fourteenth century, it was used to describe a dog bite or an attempt by a dog to bite. It was the equivalent of a dog "snapping" at you.

By the eighteenth century, this verb had become a noun that meant "a small bit of food." The leap most likely was made because, if a dog got a piece of you, it wouldn't be a whole lot because you'd be running away. Or, maybe the new meaning of "snack" suggested the rapid snapping of a dog at your heels or fingers. A snack, after all, is usually consumed quickly.

By the nineteenth century, the word regained its definition as a verb but with a new meaning. Nowadays, this word can be either a noun or verb, depending on context.

---

sneer

ORIGINAL DEFINITION: to snort, as a horse or dog
NEW DEFINITION: curl one's lip to show disdain

S

"Sneer" is an example of both onomatopoeia and reverse personification. "Onomatopoeia" is that fancy and hard-to-spell term to describe words that imitate sounds. Personification occurs when you give nonhuman things or animals human characteristics. In this case, human beings actually got "sneer" from the animals.

Originally, "sneer" was used to describe the snorting of a horse or dog. When a horse snorts, it does sound reminiscent of a person puffing out her lips in scorn. Some of the words that are the origins of "sneer" most likely were coined due their imitative, or onomatopoeic, nature.

Another of "sneer's" origin words means "grin like a dog," which probably explains how curling one's lip became necessary for demonstrating scorn. Thus, when Elvis Presley showed off his famous sneer, he wasn't acting like nothin' but a hound dog.

---

soap box

ORIGINAL DEFINITION: box holding soap
NEW DEFINITION: improvised platform—sometimes real, sometimes metaphorical—on which one pontificates

When "soap box" first began to appear in writing during the seventeenth century, it referred to a box in which one carried soap.

Since soap existed as much as 3,000 years before Christ, "soap box" or some variation was probably used even longer ago in conversation. "Hey, Ramses, where do you want these soap boxes?"

Leave the pharaohs behind and move forward some 5,000 years to the days just before World War I. Many people were out of work. Popular entertainment options were limited. Many new political movements were in the air. And cardboard hadn't been invented yet.

Prior to the familiar cardboard box, manufacturers used sturdy, wooden crates for shipping. As a result, "soap boxes" were easily available. People with time on their hands, no TV to watch, and a desire to spread the word about the offbeat political movement "du jour," grabbed a box, set it up on the corner of a public street, and started orating their guts out.

Presumably, soup box or cantaloupe box could have caught on instead of soap box. Perhaps "soap" became the favored box because people stood on these platforms and "cleared the air."

—— *Soap Box Derby* ——

Since the 1930s, people have made cars out of various household objects—without motors, engines, etc.—and let gravity carry them down a hill until one of the cars crosses the finish line first.

Ironically, no one—even the All-American Soap Box Derby (AASBD), which governs the annual All-American Race—knows why "soap box" became the type of box associated with the derby. The organization's website notes that plenty of orange crates were used in the early days and suggests that someone probably just randomly used a soap box, but it's seemingly no more aware of the event's etymological origins than the average derby competitor.

sophisticated

ORIGINAL DEFINITION: one characterized by sophistry, i.e., a deceitful person

NEW DEFINITION: worldly wise and refined

Some Brits may still describe a cheeky ne'er-do-well as "sophisticated" because that's in keeping with the word's original definition. "Sophistication" suggested the use of sophistry, which was once a synonym for "wisdom." It comes from a Latin word meaning teacher or wise man. By medieval times, a "sophist" was what he or she is today: someone who talks a good game but uses pretty words to cheat others out of money, sex, or goods, or to get others to do their bidding. Think, for example, of Charles Manson. His rhetoric was laced with all the 1960s-era platitudes, but underneath, his words were weapons. Thus, from the fourteenth century until the nineteenth century, you would not have wanted to be called "sophisticated."

By the middle of the nineteenth century, however, "sophisticated" gained a new lease on life. It went back to its roots and suggested wisdom . . . but with a modern twist. As people became more aware of cultures beyond their own and grew more literate, that old chestnut, "sophisticated," was brushed off and used to describe people who have attained a degree of worldly wisdom and a patina of refinement.

S

spinster

ORIGINAL DEFINITION: a woman who spins thread
NEW DEFINITION: a woman who remains single beyond the typical age for marrying

It's no surprise that sexism plays a big part in this largely discarded word, which is still occasionally used to describe women who remain single into menopause.

In the 1300s and well into the 1600s, a "spinster" was simply a woman who spun or worked with thread for a living. Spinning was one of the few careers available for women. Of course, in those days, most women only worked until they were "rescued" from labor by a husband.

Some women were still spinning at the "old age" of twenty-five, and some (probably male) wags began to refer to them as "spinsters," meaning, basically, "old maids." Some of these men were aghast at women working in the first place. Legal documents began to use the term "spinster" as a generic term for an unmarried woman. The word has fallen out of favor almost entirely today.

stadium

ORIGINAL DEFINITION: measure of length or a footrace
NEW DEFINITION: large, oval structure in which sporting events take place

Prior to the nineteenth century, no one would have understood a simple modern-day sentence like the following: "We went to the stadium and saw the game." For centuries, a "stadium" was a unit of length or perhaps a type of footrace that was a "stadium" in length.

S

The roots of "stadium" go all the way back to ancient Greece. The Greeks were physical fitness nuts. They loved footraces. A race run at a track in Olympia (site of the original Olympics) was a "stadium" in length, which is equivalent to about 600 feet. Thus, "stadium" came to mean both the length and the race itself.

Even after "stadium" entered English—sometime in the fourteenth century—it still had these dual meanings. By the seventeenth century, however, "stadium" was used generically to mean a running track of any length. And then, in the nineteenth century, large, open-air venues for sports—often containing running tracks—began to be referred to as stadiums.

These days, only a professor of antiquities would make a direct connection between "stadium" and "footrace" or "stadium" and "unit measurement," for that matter.

S

— *The Only Two Still Standing* —

Starting in the 1990s, baseball teams tore down historic stadiums and replaced them with new, modern facilities. Even the venerable Yankee Stadium got replaced in 2009. Only two classic baseball stadiums remain . . . unless one of them has been imploded by the time you read this.

The oldest stadium is Boston's Fenway Park. The Red Sox have played there since 1912. Compared to recently built parks, Fenway's size barely qualifies it as a stadium. For one thing, it's irregularly shaped. For another, its seating capacity is just over 37,400. (The new, improved Yankee Stadium, by contrast, holds more than 52,000.)

The second-oldest baseball stadium is Chicago's Wrigley Field. It was not always home to the seemingly ill-fated Chicago Cubs. The stadium opened in 1914 and was home to the Chicago Whales of the short-lived Federal League. The Cubs moved there in 1916 and The Loveable Losers have been making fans cry ever since.

starve

ORIGINAL DEFINITION: to die
NEW DEFINITION: to die, specifically from lack of food

For centuries, no one would have used the now common expression, "starve to death" because it would have been redundant. "Starve," from a root meaning "stiff," simply meant "to die." Thus, you could "starve" due to everything from the bubonic plague to an unlucky accident involving an angry horse.

During the Middle English period, the word began to shift. For the fourteenth and fifteenth centuries, "starve" meant to die of hypothermia. It was equivalent to dying of exposure. As Middle English gave way to Modern English, the word began its final transformation to "death by hunger."

A possibility for why the new meaning of "starve" is restricted to hunger is that, for most of its life, "starve" carried with it the suggestion of a slow death, a wasting away. Extreme hunger causes just such a death. After reading this grim description, you should go gorge on a gallon Ben & Jerry's.

stew

ORIGINAL DEFINITION: vessel for cooking; cauldron
NEW DEFINITION: meat and vegetables in a broth

"Stew" has an interesting history. For one thing, it's a word that underwent a metonymic shift, and for another, it spent part of its life in houses of ill repute.

As noted elsewhere, metonymy occurs when you refer to one thing because it's associated with something else. For example, athletes are called jocks because male ones wore jockstraps. One says the kettle is boiling, but it's actually the water *in* the kettle that's boiling.

Once upon a time, a "stew" was a cauldron. Picture Shakespeare's weird sisters (see entry for "weird") stirring the pot and saying, "Bubble, bubble, toil and trouble." Then, as now, an easy meal consisted of throwing a bunch of meat and vegetables into a pot and letting it boil for a while. Eventually, this meal *cooked* in the "stew" *became* stew.

"Stew" also used to be a verb meaning "to marinate in a steam bath." Apparently, brothels of the Middle Ages were known for offering this kind of "stew" (as well as many other earthly delights). Thus, for a period, brothels were known as "stews"— another example of metonymy.

S

stogie

ORIGINAL DEFINITION: shoe
NEW DEFINITION: cheap cigar

Did you know there's a connection between cheap cigars and the taming of the Wild West?

Conestoga wagons, named for the Pennsylvania county in which they were built, first began trekking across America fifty years before the American Revolution. Long before they rolled across the prairies of Kansas and the Dakotas, Conestogas "tamed" the Appalachian region. After the Revolution, Conestogas tamed Ohio, which *was* the West at that time.

Ultimately, Conestogas found themselves out in the "real" West. These are the wagons Americans tend to picture when they think of "covered wagons." Conestogas were designed to be mostly waterproof when crossing streams, and they could carry loads up to eight tons.

During the California Gold Rush, which began in 1848, Conestogas were practically as common as prairie grass. Folks began to ascribe all sorts of quirks to those who preferred Conestoga wagons as their conveyances of choice.

For one thing, men who drove Conestogas typically wore thick-soled shoes. People began to refer to these shoes as "stogies," short for Conestoga. A few decades later, people—likely with clucking tongues—also began to refer to the cheap cigars favored by Conestoga drivers as "stogies." The "shoe" meaning has largely disappeared, but big, cheap, odorous cigars are still called stogies.

S

stooge

ORIGINAL DEFINITION: a stagehand
NEW DEFINITION: someone who assists others in, typically, nefarious enterprises

A "stooge" was originally a stagehand. The word had existed in vaudeville since the early twentieth century.

Of course, when you hear "stooge" today, it's impossible not to think of The Three Stooges. Originally, this comedy troupe—known for its eye-gouging and nyuk, nyuk, nyuks—was called Ted Healy and His Stooges. Healy was the leader of the group, and the shtick was that, while he tried to sing or tell jokes, his noisy stagehands—or stooges—would interrupt him. Before long, The Three Stooges stole the show, leaving people to ask, "Who's Ted Healy?"

Some etymologists believe the word "stooge" began to change in meaning because of The Three Stooges. And here you thought there was nothing remotely culturally relevant about the group!

This shift helped the word "stooge" reach its principal modern meaning: a none-too-bright lackey, or someone who allows herself or her company to be used to help, say, big business. The suggestion that someone is a "stooge" for the oil industry packs a mighty, pejorative sting.

—— *Other Stooges* ——

Comedy teams often feature one member who's bizarre, kooky, or silly (Jerry Lewis, Lou Costello) and one who seems reasonably sedate and normal (Dean Martin, Bud Abbott). This "normal" member of the team is sometimes called a stooge. He's also called a "feed," "dead wood," or a "straight man."

Another type of stooge is someone who helps a magician. Sometimes a magician will pull a spectator out of the crowd to take part in a trick. Often, the person really is just a spectator. At other times, however, he or she is a stooge, someone who secretly is working with the magician to make the trick take place successfully.

Finally, there's an algorithm called a Stooge sort. The algorithm is used in computer programming to swap values around, causing them to "knock into" each other. The Stooge sort actually was named for The Three Stooges, who often hit each other during their routines.

stove

ORIGINAL DEFINITION: steam room
NEW DEFINITION: device for cooking food

At the outset of its lexical life, "stove" meant steam room or bath room, i.e., room in which one takes a steam bath. Thus, one sweated one's cares away in the "stove." One also, most likely, met casual sexual partners in the "stove." Steam baths of the Middle

Ages often doubled as brothels and frequently included "bath rooms" as part of their fare.

By the seventeenth century, "stove" stopped being a steam room and became the well-known cooking device. The connection makes sense. Both a steam room and a cooking device heat things up . . . especially when that steam room doubles as a brothel. Then you're really cookin'.

Some Brits still call greenhouses "stoves," which may seem odd at first, but the word keeps alive "stove's" original definition.

S

—— *Stove Pipe Hats* ——

The term "stove pipes" (meaning, simply, thick black pipes connected to a stove) came along by the end of the 1600s. By the 1850s, stoves— and stove pipes—were so well-known that they lent their name to a similar-looking popular style of gentleman's hat, which President Abraham Lincoln made forever famous.

success

ORIGINAL DEFINITION: outcome; result (not necessarily positive)
NEW DEFINITION: attainment of a desired or hoped-for outcome

At one time, "success" wasn't about achieving desired ends. It was a synonym for "result"—sometimes good, sometimes bad, sometimes a little of both. Your crops were plentiful? "Success." Your crops all died? "Success."

The Latin word from which "success" springs contains an element of "happy outcome." Think, for example, of the word "succession." Something leads to something else. The result, as often as not, is positive. Of course, sometimes succession—of a president, for example—occurs because of an untimely death.

Ultimately, by the seventeenth century, "success" became associated specifically with the fulfillment of a positive, desired end. As early as the turn of the twentieth century, psychology pioneer William James diagnosed America's main małady: too much attention to the "bitch-goddess Success." That's America! We want to be first! We want to be the best! We want to be better than our neighbors! We want every piece of the pie! Thus, one's Middle English ancestors paved the way for modern-day Americans to chase after that particular "bitch-goddess" with all the gusto they can manage.

S

---

symposium

ORIGINAL DEFINITION: drinking party (fun)
NEW DEFINITION: conference focused on a particular topic (not fun)

"Symposium's" roots actually mean "gather and drink." Romans and Greeks alike enjoyed—*seriously* enjoyed—"symposia" (the Romans called them "convivia" . . . but same thing). Picture Plato's version as a bevy of MENSA members congregating to play beer pong while having intellectual conversations. His concept of a "symposium" translated well into English and remained intact well into the eighteenth century.

Then colleges and universities began to take the fun out of "symposia." They borrowed the word and (sort of) the concept of a symposium by gathering people together to discuss arcane topics. If you've ever been to a symposium, then you know the word's true definition should be "embodiment of boredom." Symposia are an excuse for eggheads to congregate, lay a few ideas, cluck their tongues in opposition, and go back home to roost.

Thus, by the nineteenth century, symposia were stripped of all their earlier, enjoyable elements. They became excuses to go to a university in the middle of nowhere, and listen to a bunch of people ramble, sadly, without beer pong.

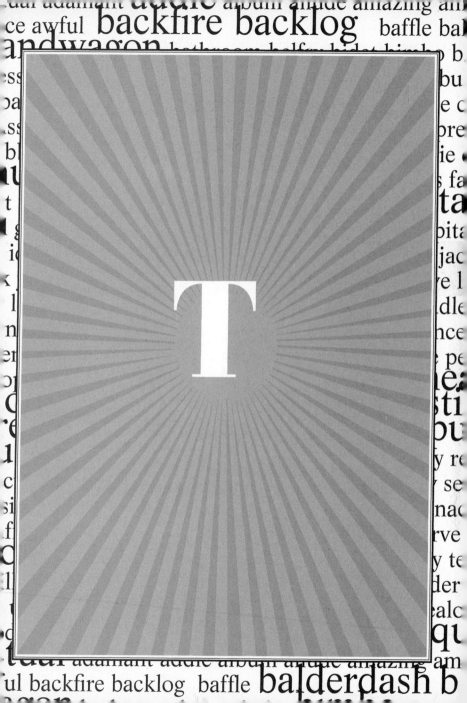

tawdry

ORIGINAL DEFINITION: lace ribbon for a lady's neck
NEW DEFINITION: cheap; gaudy

St. Awdrey, as she's generally known, founded a monastery in 673 in a village called Ely, near Cambridge, England. For centuries, an annual fair held in the village to honor the saint was known for its modest lacework decorations, which ladies of the day wore about their necks.

As time went on, the simple lacework became, well, gaudier. Or at least the Puritans thought so. (Honestly! They took the fun out of everything!) They descried St. Awdrey's lace, and eventually "St. Awdrey" transformed into "tawdry." Thus, the same folks who brought America witch trials and scarlet letters also bequeathed to the English language a word that still means cheap, showy, and gaudy.

termagant

ORIGINAL DEFINITION: fictional Muslim deity
NEW DEFINITION: quarrelsome, scolding woman

During the Middle Ages, most people couldn't read, but they were still expected to know the Bible . . . or at least the highlights of the Bible. If people couldn't read, then how did the clergy bring the Word of God to the masses? They created mystery plays, so called because they featured the mysteries (i.e., miracles) of Christ's life.

Then, as now, however, those who put on plays aimed at the "rabble" knew they had to throw the common folks bones. They couldn't just offer strict theology because it would have bored the very folks performers tried to reach. One way to appease the masses was through farce (see entry for "farce"), and another was the creation of over-the-top villains (see entry for "villain").

Herod was a favorite villain. In case you've forgotten, he was the king who tried to kill the baby Jesus. Another bad guy of choice was completely fictional. His name originally was Tervagant, but this switched later to Termagant.

Termagant was a fictional Muslim deity. You see, Christians didn't know much about Muslims during the Middle Ages. They just knew Muslims were evil . . . because the clergy told them so. Most people had no idea how Muslims worshipped, so they created Termagant to fill that void. This fictional god yelled, screamed, and overacted just as much as Herod.

Over time, "termagant" (with a lower-case "t") came to denote anyone—male or female—who is quarrelsome or extremely disagreeable. Ultimately, the word became almost entirely associated with stereotypical depictions of yelling, screaming, quarrelsome women.

T

---

test

ORIGINAL DEFINITION: cupel
NEW DEFINITION: trial; examination

What? You don't know what a "cupel" is? You would have known if you'd lived during the fourteenth century and wanted to get your money's worth.

A "cupel," also called a "test," was used to assay precious metals. The "test" was a porous cup into which one poured molten silver or gold. Impurities in the valuable minerals were absorbed by the "test," leaving pure gold and silver. Thus was born the expression, "put something to the test."

By the seventeenth century, writers borrowed "test" and made it into a metaphor. The "test" "examined" the gold and filtered impurities from it, so a "test" became a general word for examination or trial. As other means of purifying precious metals became available, the "cupel" fell out of use, leaving behind the "test" we know today.

thrill

ORIGINAL DEFINITION: to pierce, as with an arrow
NEW DEFINITION: to excite; cause a shudder of emotion

In the 1300s, "thrill" meant to pierce or penetrate. For example, if you were on the battlefield, and a spear went through your guts, you were "thrilled." The word's roots hearken back to "hole," which is what you'll have if something pierces you.

By the turn of the seventeenth century, writers already were starting to use "thrill" in a metaphorical sense. Rather than being pierced by an arrow, someone "thrilled" was "pierced" by an emotional overload. If you've experienced the thrill of love, then you know it's a visceral feeling. Literally, you shudder, flooded with a myriad of emotions you can't process. No wonder Cupid comes equipped with a quiver. When love "hits" you, you feel like you've been pierced by an arrow. That feeling is how the word "thrill" changed in meaning. The word became a noun by the eighteenth century, and in the twentieth century, it came to mean "an experience that is exciting."

tinker

ORIGINAL DEFINITION: mender of pots and pans
NEW DEFINITION: to work at something in an unskilled way

Long before Angie's List, people could make known their dissatisfaction with a skilled worker. Take the example of the "tinker" for proof. In the Middle Ages, a "tinker" was an itinerant (mobile) mender of household items such as pots, pans, and kettles. The word may derive from the sound a "tinker" made when hammering on metallic items.

But notice that key word: "itinerant." These folks ambled into town, claimed to be excellent menders, and often left behind shoddy craftsmanship. By the time the folks in the household realized they'd thrown money away on a faulty job, these "tinkers" were long gone.

Thus, unskilled labor masquerading as skilled labor played a part in the transformation of "tinker" from a word with a neutral connotation to one with a negative connotation. All dissatisfied customers on Angie's List can do is give plumbers negative reviews, but folks who got irritated with "tinkers" caused the word "tinker" to adopt an entirely new meaning.

T

—— *Tinker's Damn* ——

Not only were "tinkers" lousy at mending, but they also had a reputation for profanity. Many claim that's the origin of the expression "tinker's damn," which means, basically, "the least amount of effort one can put into something."

Others claim that this unfairly maligns "tinkers" . . . at least the part about them being profane. For these etymologists, the expression actually is a "tinker's dam" without the blaspheming "n" at the end of the second word. A "tinker's dam" is a small plug used to help create cast metal molds. Since the plug is fairly insignificant, the expression still denotes "the least amount one can put into something."

toady

ORIGINAL DEFINITION: one who eats toads
NEW DEFINITION: servile follower

"Toady" is short for "toadeater," and that's really what the word meant in the seventeenth century. "Toadeaters," or "toadies," worked with charlatans (see entry for "charlatan"). Charlatans were quacks who sold "medicine" they claimed could cure any disease known to humankind. In fact, they could even counter the poison of toads! (In those days, people believed that toads were deadly poisonous. They feared accidentally consuming a toad's leg instead of a frog's leg.)

A charlatan's "toady" would, literally, eat a toad and then put on a smashing display of convulsions and death throes. Then, armed with his magic potion, the charlatan would bring the toady back to the pink of health.

By the eighteenth century, most people knew to avoid buying a charlatan's nostrums. But people remembered the sight of the quivering, shaking, quaking, bowing, scraping "toady." The word lost its direct association with toads and became, instead, a slavish follower, someone who would even eat a toad for his or her boss.

tomboy

ORIGINAL DEFINITION: a rude, boisterous boy
NEW DEFINITION: a girl who acts and dresses like a boy

The word "tomboy" first appeared in the early sixteenth century. At first, a "tomboy" truly was a boy, the sort who might skip school, not do his chores, get into fights, etc. He wasn't evil, just high-spirited.

The word "tom" had denoted a simple-minded person since the 1400s, and that helped give these boisterous lads their nickname: They acted like fools.

By the 1600s, "tomboys" changed gender. They were spunky girls who acted in ways one often associates with boys. They liked playing in mud, wearing pants, skipping school, etc.

A likely reason for this gender change is that the word "tomboy" derives not from the boys' nickname "tom" but from an Anglo-Saxon word meaning "dancer" or "one who tumbles about." This led the word to be associated with prostitutes, who, um, like to tumble about.

Eventually, the high-spirited tumbling simply became high spirits, the opposite of the meekness with which one associated girls for centuries. Thus, the word had a pejorative ring. Most tomboys today are proud to be assertive and not "girly girls," but the word can still be used as an insult.

T

---

truant

ORIGINAL DEFINITION: beggar
NEW DEFINITION: one who disregards a duty, especially one who skips school

At one time, a "truant" was a beggar, a vagabond, one who wandered from place to place entreating strangers for a crust of sustaining bread.

"Truant's" origins include words referring to everything from beggars to scoundrels to buffoons (see entry for "buffoon"). In other words, the suggestion was that these people *chose* to be beggars or ludicrous figures (see entry for "ludicrous"). They weren't out on the streets due to bad luck, rather, to bad choices.

The modern truant is known for his (usually "his") poor choices and for his buffoonish behavior. It's most often used to describe children who skip school.

umpire

ORIGINAL DEFINITION: from "noumper," meaning odd, as in, not even
NEW DEFINITION: decision maker during sporting events

Like the word "apron" (see entry for "apron"), "umpire" not only once had a different meaning, it had an entirely different spelling.

The French word that gave rise to "umpire" starts with an "n." But when it got translated into English, people misheard the word. Instead of hearing "un noumper," most thought the word was "un oumper." Thus, after a few more spelling shifts, the word "umpire" forever lost the "n" with which it should begin.

Now, for the meaning change. Umpire, or "noumper," meant "an odd number," but it was used primarily as a word related to a third party who settles disputes between two parties. For example, say two guys are fighting over a property boundary. A third is brought in to make an impartial decision about the situation. This "odd man" was the "noumper."

Since the word already suggested someone who settles arguments, it came to be used in sporting events, which often have disputed plays. Umpires, without their "n's," were first used (or at least first called umpires) during boxing matches in the eighteenth century.

undertaker

ORIGINAL DEFINITION: businessman
NEW DEFINITION: funeral director; mortician

Historically, an "undertaker" was any entrepreneur or businessperson. The word comes from the noun "undertake," which means "take on responsibility." If you were an "undertaker," you were a go-getter, a self-starter, a real live wire.

One specific type of undertaker was the "funeral undertaker," but, presumably, there were "millinery undertakers" or "cobbler undertakers" or "what-have-you undertakers" throughout the English-speaking world.

Most likely, the reason for the change in definition was short life spans. At a time when the average life span was forty—thanks to all manner of diseases, plagues, and epidemics—"funeral undertakers" were busier than many other "undertakers." Eventually, as the word came to be associated mostly with practitioners of the "mortal arts," other "undertakers" steered away from the name. The transformation of "undertaker" to mean "mortician" was complete by the eighteenth century.

Nowadays, the only undertaker who doesn't embalm corpses is Mark Calaway, a professional wrestler who goes by the name "The Undertaker," and who dresses like some sort of demon from the Wild West.

U

unfair

ORIGINAL DEFINITION: ugly
NEW DEFINITION: not just; not equitable

The Old English word from which "unfair" derives meant "ugly." A maiden with whom no one wanted to dance around a Maypole was "unfair."

The word took a slight metaphorical jump during the Middle Ages. "Ugly" already could refer to more than just looks, so something "unfair" became something vile and contemptible. It was "ugly" as in an "ugly fight," "ugly situation," an "ugly mess."

By the eighteenth century, "unfair" no longer had such an evil connotation. It softened a bit to the word used today by every teenager who's ever been told she can't borrow the car because she got a D in English class.

U

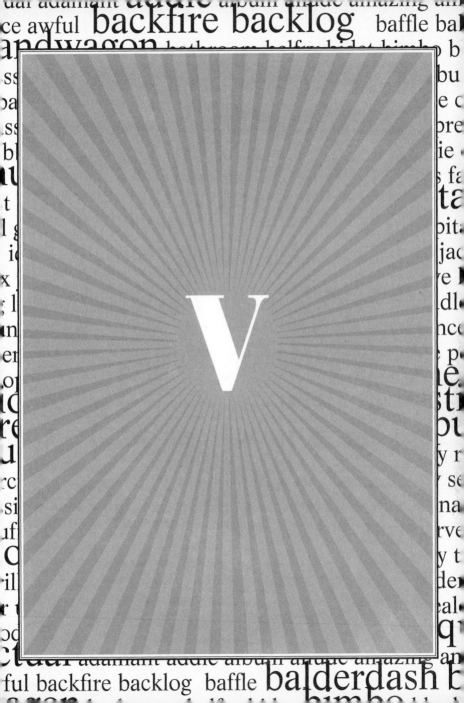

vibrant

ORIGINAL DEFINITION: agitated; edgy
NEW DEFINITION: lively

In the mid-sixteenth century, "vibrant" meant agitated. It came from the same root as "vibrate." Someone "vibrant" seemed to be vibrating internally, ready at any moment to explode into sense-less rage or a neurotic rant. He was edgy and filled a room with negative energy.

Over the next 300 years, the word "vibrant" did what most edgy people never do: It actually chilled out. The word gradually lost its negative connotation and came to describe people who are full of life and always seem in motion. After all, that's what "agi-tate" technically means: to move rapidly.

---

villain

ORIGINAL DEFINITION: someone from the country; someone poor; someone "low-born"
NEW DEFINITION: a bad guy in a book, movie, play, etc.

V

Class-consciousness is not a modern invention. There have always been "one-percenters," as the word "villain" proves.

Originally, "villain" referred to someone from a farm or a small village: a hayseed, a yahoo, a bumpkin. Most likely, this "villain" didn't have much money. He didn't have impeccable manners. He belched and farted and drank too much elderberry wine. In short: he wasn't a bad guy, just someone with coarse manners and not much coin.

Soon after the word began to appear in the 1300s, it began to take on a more distinctly pejorative connotation. Someone poor and uncultured became associated with someone base and immoral. Thus, a "villain" wasn't just someone from "the sticks," he was someone vile and loathsome.

By the early nineteenth century, "villain" lost all connection to harmless rustics and referred exclusively to miscreants (see entry for "miscreant"), rapscallions, reprobates, and guys in black cowboy hats.

V

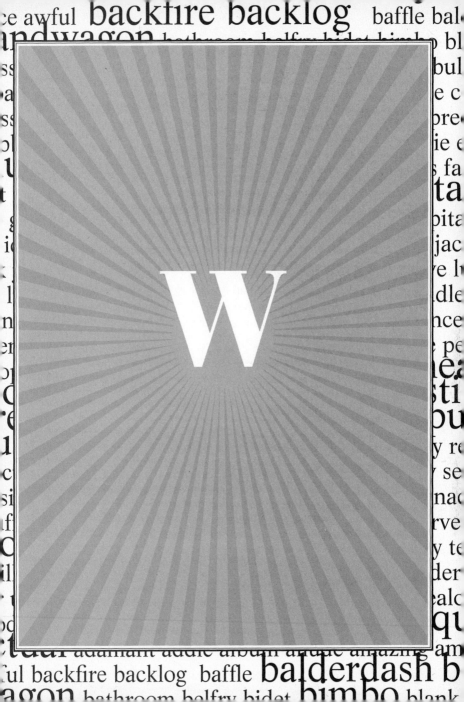

W

weird

ORIGINAL DEFINITION: fate; destiny
NEW DEFINITION: unusual; odd

Fans of the Bard probably assume that the three "weird sisters" who plant ideas in Macbeth's head are ugly, scary, weird-looking hags. But they were called "weird" because in Shakespeare's day, "weird" was related to fate or destiny. The sisters were "weird" because they could foretell Macbeth's future.

In fact, Shakespeare didn't invent the "weird sisters"; they can be found throughout Middle English literature. They are the "three fates" who determine human destiny. However, since they almost invariably are described as looking like stereotypical witches, the term "weird" ultimately began to take on its modern-day meaning of "bizarre" or "uncanny."

By the middle of the nineteenth century, the original meaning of "weird" had nearly faded away. And now most productions of *Macbeth* feature "weird sisters" who look, well, weird and scary.

—— *It's Uncanny!* ——

A word related to "weird" that also has undergone some changes is "uncanny." Originally, the word meant "mischievous." "Canny" means careful, prudent, and cautious; thus, someone "uncanny" is none of those things and is therefore mischievous.

By the eighteenth century, "uncanny" had become a synonym for "weird," "strange," and "mysteriously unsettling." For most, the only time you ever hear the word is when someone is described as having an "uncanny resemblance" to someone—often a celebrity, a relative from several generations back, or even a complete stranger.

From the 1930s to the 1960s, the actor William Henry Pratt was so well known for his signature horror roles that he was often described ➤

W

as uncanny. Better known by his stage name, Boris Karloff, "Karloff the Uncanny" played the quintessential "weird and unsettling" parts of Frankenstein's monster and the mummy.

wistful

ORIGINAL DEFINITION: attentive; focused
NEW DEFINITION: sadly yearning

In the seventeenth century, "wistful" derived from an older word that meant "intent." Thus, the word could describe what we today call a "stalker." You could be "wistful"—intent, focused—on someone's wife. Think of F. Scott Fitzgerald's *The Great Gatsby*—Gatsby was "wistful" on Daisy Buchanan.

Over time, the word "wistful" dropped its origin word and got adopted by the word "wishful." By the eighteenth century, the "stalker" connotation was gone, and the word came to mean "marked by wishing for something one probably cannot get." Thus, you can be wistful about a romantic interest from the past, just as Gatsby is wistful about Daisy . . . to the point of stalking her to East Egg, New York.

wizard

ORIGINAL DEFINITION: a wise man; a sage
NEW DEFINITION: a magician; a sorcerer; one who "works magic" on objects like computers that stymie many of us

In the Middle Ages, magic and science were practically conjoined twins. It was difficult to ascertain where one ended and the other

W

began. Thus, "wizard" derives from a word that means "wise" and probably referred to men who could foretell the future.

If you believed then—as many did—that prognostication was a science and not a parlor trick, then you would think a "wizard" was exceedingly wise. By the end of the Middle Ages, many people stopped believing in the validity of soothsayers but not, apparently, in the reality of magic. In 1600, "wizards" referred to those who had magical powers. By the early 1900s, most wizards could only be found in storybooks, such as L. Frank Baum's about the merry old Land of Oz.

Both senses of the word exist when you call someone a "wizard" at math or physics or computers. While we struggle, they make difficult stuff look easy. They're so wise, it's like magic!

W

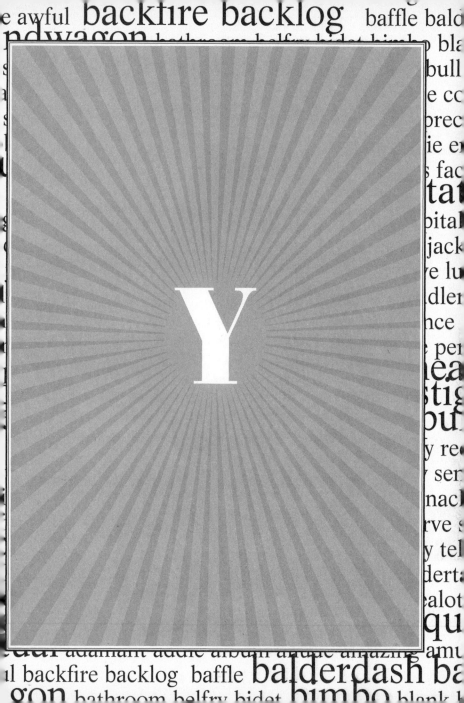

yen

Y

ORIGINAL DEFINITION: craving for opium (often written as yen-yen)

NEW DEFINITION: strong desire; yearning

No one speaks of a drug addict having a yen for heroin. "Yen" suggests a yearning, not a need. Therefore, we use the word "addiction" for those who crave drugs. Yet, when the word first entered English it was related specifically to opium addiction.

During the eighteenth and nineteenth centuries, traders made huge profits getting Chinese peasants addicted to opium. In part, the attraction to opium resulted from a ban on tobacco imposed by the emperor during the seventeenth century. As large numbers of Chinese immigrated to the United States, some brought their addiction with them . . . as well as the word "in-yan," which described it.

To Americans, the Chinese word sounded like "yen-yen," so that is what the word for opium addiction became in English. Ultimately, the second "yen" was dropped. Gradually, the word lost its explicit connection to opium addiction and became instead a word for strong desire.

zany

ORIGINAL DEFINITION: clown; fool
NEW DEFINITION: foolish; buffoonish

The word "zany" started out life as a clown (see entry for "clown").

The life story of "zany" begins in sixteenth-century Italy. The word actually is a diminutive of Giovanni, or John, in English. A "zany" was a stock character of the Italian stage. He would wander amid the principal actors and mock or imitate them.

Think, for example, of how you used to imitate your little sister in order to make her cry. A "zany" was something like that. Sounds annoying, but it was a common character, so people of the day must have loved their zanies.

The word began to fade but gained a new lease on life in the nineteenth century. It stopped being a noun. In those days, "zanies" as characters were out of favor; thus, "zany" took on a new existence as an adjective that might have described those old stock characters.

Bibliography

Anxiety and Depression Association of America. *www.adaa.org/ understanding-anxiety.*

Asimov, Isaac. *Words from History.* (Boston, MA: Houghton Mifflin Company, 1968).

Brainy Quote. *www.brainyquote.com.*

Burridge, Kate. *Blooming English: Observations on the Roots, Cultivation, and Hybrids of the English language.* (New York, NY: Cambridge University Press, 2004).

Carver, Craig M. *A History of English in Its Own Words.* (New York, NY: HarperCollins Publishers, 1991).

Cooper, Barbara Roisman. "John Logie Baird: Forgotten Pioneer of Television." *www.historynet.com/john-logie-baird-forgotten-pioneer-of-television.htm.*

Discordian Wiki. *http://discordia.wikia.com/wiki/The_Aftermath.*

Doyle, Gabe. "Some Words Whose Meanings Have Changed Without Controversy." *http://motivatedgrammar.wordpress.com/2010/01/28/ some-words-whose-meanings-have-changed-without-controversy/.*

"Dumpster Diving." *http://theeconomiccollapseblog.com/archives/ dumpster-diving.*

Editors, Merriam-Webster. *Webster's Dictionary of Word Origins.* (New York, NY: Smithmark Publishers, 1995).

"Euphemisms for Death." *www.you-can-be-funny.com/Euphemisms-For-Death .html.*

Funk, Wilfred. *Word Origins and Their Romantic Stories.* (New York, NY: Bell Publishing Company, 1950).

Gersh-Nesic, Beth. "Pop Art—Art History 101 Basics." *http://arthistory .about.com/od/modernarthistory/a/Pop-Art-Art-History-101-Basics.htm.*

"Gout stools." *www.ebay.com/sch/i.html?_from=R40&_trksid=p5197.m570 .l1313&_nkw=gout+stool&_sacat=See-All-Categories.*

Harper, Douglas. Online Etymology Dictionary. *www.etymonline.com.*

Heckle Depot. *www.heckledepot.com.*

The Internet Movie Database. *www.imdb.com/title/tt0057733/.*

Keyes, Ralph. *Euphemania: Our Love Affair with Euphemisms.* (New York, NY: Little, Brown and Company, 2010).

KryssTal. "The Origin of Words and Names." *www.krysstal.com/wordname .html.*

Lienhard, John H. "Thoreau's Pencils." *www.uh.edu/engines/epi339.htm.*

Merriam-Webster. *www.merriam-webster.com.*

Mikkelson, Barbara. "Shit Faced." *www.snopes.com/language/acronyms/shit .asp.*

Novobatzky, Peter and Ammon Shea. *Depraved and Insulting English.* (New York, NY: Harvest, 2001).

Purple Priestess. "The Mad Logophile: Words That Have Changed Their Meaning: Part 1." *The Daily Kos. www.dailykos.com/ story/2009/05/31/735843/-The-Mad-Logophile-Words-That-Have-Changed-Their-Meaning-Part-1.*

———. "The Mad Logophile: Words That Have Changed Their Meaning: Part 2." *The Daily Kos. www.dailykos.com/story/2009/06/07/736893/-The-Mad-Logophile-Words-That-Have-Changed-Their-Meaning-Part-2.*

Swall, Andrian. "Eight Words Which Have Completely Changed Their Meaning Over Time." *http://writinghood.com/style/grammar/ eight-words-which-have-completely-changed-their-meaning-over-time/.*

Wikipedia: The Free Encyclopedia. *http://en.wikipedia.org/wiki/Main_Page.*

Wiktionary, the Free Dictionary. *http://en.wiktionary.org/wiki/ Wiktionary:Main_Page.*